AF413433

NEVER TELL
A BLACK
GIRL
HOW TO
BLACK GIRL

NEVER TELL A BLACK GIRL HOW TO BLACK GIRL

ESSAYS

AMENA BROWN

An imprint of Penguin Random House LLC
1745 Broadway, New York, NY 10019
penguinrandomhouse.com

Tiny Reparations and Tiny Reparations Books with colophon are registered trademarks of YQY, Inc.

"Our Own Potluck" was originally published on whetstonemagazine.com in 2020. Used by permission of the author.

BOOK DESIGN BY ANGIE BOUTIN

LIBRARY OF CONGRESS CATALOGING-IN-PUBLICATION DATA
has been applied for.

ISBN 9798217044689 (hardcover)
ISBN 9798217044702 (ebook)

Printed in the United States of America
1st Printing

The authorized representative in the EU for product safety and compliance is Penguin Random House Ireland, Morrison Chambers, 32 Nassau Street, Dublin D02 YH68, Ireland, https://eu-contact.penguin.ie.

To my sister bestie, Makeda,
for all the ways you Black Girl
for all the ways we Black Girl together

CONTENTS

INTRODUCTION

lack Girl is a noun and a verb. I am a Black girl and I Black Girl. I am a Black girl raised mostly in the South and I Black Girl by always needing to have enough oil in my house to fry chicken just in case. I am a Black girl who loves cheese fries and I Black Girl by requiring myself to answer, "YES INDEED," anytime Lil' Kim asks, "Shall I proceed?"

We all Black Girl in different ways. Black women are a whole world. To me, it's as if there is an entire stratosphere of *just us*. A solar system of customs, languages, codes, unspoken understandings. A galaxy of Black-woman-ness and what it means to be who we are, where we are, during the time in which we live. Being a Black woman is beautiful, it's gorgeous, it's full of joy and soul. There is elasticity in the way we express ourselves, so much so that I could never speak for all Black women or know every one of our perspectives. The fullness of who we are cannot be contained in one book, one poem, one story. We are too vast and layered and diasporic for that. So, I will tell my own Black girl stories, to share about my corner of the world, in hopes that you will find echoes of your own stories, stories of people you know or stories that broaden what you think you know.

I have Black Girled in six countries and over half of the fifty states. I learned about how to Black Girl in my great-grandmother's backyard as she hung clothes on the line, in my grandmother's kitchen as she fried chicken, in my mother's kitchen as she placed the pressing comb on the eye of the stove. I experienced the many ways a Black girl can Black Girl at my alma mater Spelman College, which felt in so many ways like the International Black Girl Headquarters. I have Black Girled onstage performing poetry and telling funny stories. I Black Girled with Janelle Monáe in their "Tightrope" music video. I Black Girled with Tracee Ellis Ross in writing the poetic language for her hair care brand, PATTERN Beauty. I have Black Girled at three of Beyoncé's concerts, in several beauty supply stores, with my sister in art galleries and in gas stations, in sexy heels and in my freshest sneakers.

In this book of essays, poems, stories, and random lists, I will share lessons I've learned in a Black hair salon, underwear mishaps, why I love my Black woman therapist, what being broke taught me about food and relationships, why every Angry Black Woman deserves a playlist, and why no one should ever tell a Black girl how to Black Girl.

Here, I share the fact that I am not my hair, but in some ways I am. My hair and I switch up style and shape, and we both refuse to be dry and ashy. I celebrate back fat and cellulite. I earned both with the same vigor I earned my Girl Scout badges! I share that I love to cook, but more than that I love to eat. I make the mac and cheese in my family, and I will drive to the ends of the earth for the right plate of carbohydrates. I love a four-star hotel and I love a hole-in-the-wall restaurant. I share that I fell in love and got married, and my husband accepts and is well aware of who is on my fantasy "Could Get It" list.

My perspectives in this book were heavily influenced by watching hours of *Real Housewives*, my long talks with my plants and my dog where I was convinced they could both talk back to me, my commitment to cake, and the things I found funny even when life was not funny at all.

My brain is a running archive of gospel music, church sayings, lines from *I'm Gonna Git You Sucka* and *The Color Purple*, random raps from the 1990s, and at least twenty quotes from Nene Leakes, Cardi B, and Beyoncé. I read Toni Morrison and watch *Love After Lockup*. I am tender with my house plants, and I really don't like outside. I contain multitudes and contradictions, ethics and compromises, kale and donuts.

When I'm onstage I like for the audience to feel as if we are all sitting in a living room with tattered sweatpants and half-eaten snacks, having the kind of time you'd share with a friend you have deep history with. I hope you break a square off of your favorite chocolate bar, finish up the hummus you opened a week ago, and sit with these pages to laugh, breathe, think, and laugh again.

As Black women we always find a place to meet: in school, in the break room at work, in each other's kitchens and living rooms, in the natural hair product aisle, at Beyoncé concerts, in our memes, slang, facial expressions, and catchphrases that we come up with too fast for anyone to completely keep up with.

I hope this book is one of those places, a living room full of poems, stories, and belly laughs, a place to cuss and contemplate, to wonder how a well-picked afro can defy the laws of physics and why boob sweat has to exist in the first place. In these pages there will be Black girl stories and Black woman joy. There will be rhythm and rhyme and some poems that don't rhyme at all. There are so many spaces that tell a Black woman how to be, what to say, what to do, what not to do. This book is not one of them. Here, *Black Girl* is a verb. Here, we Black Girl in every way we want to.

PART 1

I WILL WEAR MY BONNET WHEREVER I WANT TO AND OTHER BLACK HAIR TALES

IT'S BEAUTIFUL TO BE A BLACK GIRL

My hair felt like an unruly friend or cousin I'd brought along with me who clearly wasn't raised right and needed constant tutelage on the rules and regulations of how to behave in summer, in winter, at church, on Easter, while playing outside, at a birthday party, before bed, in the morning immediately after waking up, and on picture day. Somehow my hair never retained any of the rules everyone spent so much time trying to teach it.

Growing up as a little Black girl in the 1980s while traveling between home with my mom in Durham, North Carolina, and my grandma's home in my mom's hometown of Goldsboro, North Carolina—there were several family discussions concerning my hair. When I stayed with my grandma for summers and holiday breaks in Goldsboro, she, my mom, and the other adult Black women had mini meetings about what they should do with my hair.

Until one day, in Durham, I experienced a hair triumph. A decision where my Black girl hair was glorious and amazing and didn't need a lecture on scruples: cornrows with beads.

I attended a Black preschool where we learned the alphabet based on Black historical figures. I distinctly remember *C* was for Crispus Attucks. There I met a little friend named Natelege, and my mom became cool with her parents to the point that I was allowed to hang out over at her place and even spend the night.

Now, a word about "spend the night." My mom, in general, didn't believe in this term. It was far off in the distance, a thing people with privilege said. To my mom, spend the night fell in the category of hearing a rich person say, "Buy whatever you want." It may be true for some people, but you shouldn't trust nearly anyone who says it to you, around you, or invites you to participate; and the people who do participate either are known and vetted family members and friends or likely have no common sense.

My mom did not believe in spend the night as a random, spontaneous occurrence. I couldn't go to the first day of school and come home to my mom and say, "Little Cassidy wants to know if I can spend the night." I couldn't go to a random playground or party with unknown children and parents and walk up to my mom, introduce her to a child and parent she never met before, and say, "Can they spend the night?"

My mom's main rule was "Don't embarrass me," and this issue fell into that category. My mom did not want to be put in a situation where she had to smile in someone's well-meaning face, knowing good and well she was never going to acquiesce to their request.

In eighteen years of a childhood, I can count on one hand

the amount of spend the nights my mom allowed. The rest of these requests were vetoed, slammed back to where they came from like a Dikembe Mutombo defense. I was allowed to spend the night with our known and vetted next-door neighbor Ms. Joan, my grandmother, my dad, and my elementary school best friend Porsha and her known and vetted parents.

All of this is to say, it was a big deal when my mom became comfortable enough with Natelege and her parents that she let me spend the night.

Natelege's mom and dad had their own garden. I was so impressed with them and loved hanging out at their house. If Natelege's mom was doing her daughter's hair, she included me too. We took turns sitting between Natelege's mom's knees, us on the floor and Natelege's mom on the couch, watching TV or playing and then being told to be still while Natelege's mom parted our hair precisely.

Natelege's mom could cornrow like nobody's business. I didn't know a lot about my hair, but Natelege's mom taught me a really cool thing my hair could do. It could handle all these parts she did with a thin comb. It could do designs with the different directions she decided to cornrow. I already loved Natelege's mom for including me in what I now know is wash day, but I wanted her to officially be a part of our family the day she put beads at the end of my cornrows.

She would pat us each on the shoulder to let us know we were done, and one by one we would find the nearest mirror and shake our heads east to west just to hear those beads click clack, to see the reflection of the light on the beads, to hear the quiet crinkle of the aluminum foil at the very ends.

There is nothing like the time in my life when I was wearing my Black little girl hair, from the plastic baubles and barrettes that held my chunky braids and plaits together to the beads and aluminum foil that punctuated my cornrows. I grew to love my Black little girl hair. I loved its texture, its curls, its naps, its kinks, the way it could defy gravity. I loved that my hair was thick. I loved how juicy my plaits were, how shiny my cornrows were.

Natelege's mom not only became the hero to my single mom (who was also trying to finish up nursing school) by saving her the time of doing my hair, but she also became my hero by saving me the stress that doing my hair had become. She showed me a beautiful thing I would experience in the homes and salon chairs of many Black women as they braided, unbraided, pressed, washed, conditioned, and styled my hair: Our hair is a part of how we care for each other and ourselves.

In the 1980s, there were so many styles Black girl hair couldn't do, but cornrows was one thing my hair could do, and I loved it! Cornrows could create an updo or a side 'do. Cornrows could give Cleo the right amount of gangsta to rob banks in *Set It Off.* Cornrows could have a Samson effect like they did on Allen Iverson's basketball prowess. Cornrows are clearly what helped Ludacris tell those people to "Rollout," "Stand Up," and "Get Back," when they ain't know him like that.

Our ancestors hid seeds of rice in their cornrows as they survived the middle passage. They designed their cornrows as maps to freedom. Cornrows hold the weight of history and the rhythm of Black girl joy. Cornrows with beads remind me of summer, jelly sandals, block parties, and cookouts. They remind me of home, family, and community. The sight of cornrows on a little Black girl is still its own hair DeLorean, reminding me how beautiful it is to be a Black girl.

IT'S JUST STEAM, BABY, AND OTHER LIES

When I was a little girl, straight hair was everything. The hair of Debbie Gibson and Brooke Shields could only be achieved with bone-straight hair. It was needed for side ponytails, for blunt bobs. For a while this didn't matter to me. I was satisfied with the barrettes and plaits and chunky twists my mom and Grandma used to style my hair. But at that time there was a moment in every Black girl's life where you would contemplate when it would be your turn to transition from your kinky and nappy hair to the land of the straight hair.

This was when there were a limited number of Black hair products to choose from to style the hair of a little girl. This was when our mamas, aunties, and grandmas used *grease*. White Rose, Blue Magic, or whichever grease the women in your family had been taught to be loyal to. There was Pink Oil Moisturizer.

Just seeing those three words makes my nostrils fill with the very distinct scent of this hair product. It smelled like "be still" and "turn your head this way" and oil mixed with a flower that doesn't exist. These were the products the adults who fixed your hair used on your non-straightened Black girl hair. You wore barrettes, plastic baubles, bobos, ponytail holders that also had different names depending on where you were from. But it was made known to you that doing your hair was no easy feat, especially if you had thick, coily hair like mine.

The adults hemmed and hawed, complained and prepared you for the long journey ahead when they would have to wash, dry, and style your hair. It wasn't a whoopin', but it felt as if they were saying it might hurt them more than it hurt you to do your hair. Which at hour two of having my hair and scalp pulled every which way, made me strongly disagree.

Then a magical moment would happen. You'd get to school, head to the playground for recess, and there would be a Black girl with long, luxurious, shiny straight hair. We'd marvel at her. Ask her how she got her hair like that, as the sun shone through the oil sheen on her tresses. She'd tell us her mama or her auntie or her big sister or her grandma or her hairdresser had straightened her hair, that we could do it too. She became a straight hair evangelist, preaching a good sermon to us, convincing us our kinky hair could also receive the salvation of a straightening comb. I could not understand the science as to how my hair, which had been categorized as thick and difficult, could so easily sway in the wind or be gathered into a ponytail when straightened.

The first time I had my hair straightened I lived with my grandma. It was my first-grade year, and my recently divorced mom had gone into the military as a nurse. Her basic training in the army required her to be away from me for almost a year, so I went to live with my grandma in Goldsboro.

My grandma was a churchgoing woman, which meant in addition to school there was a weekly event that required a hairdo and an outfit. My grandma, my hair, and I had a struggle, a tussle if you will. She needed me to "look pretty for church," which meant my hair needed to stop its unruly ways and lie down and be still. She said I was tenderheaded. I submit maybe she was heavy-handed. She even said to me one week, as I cried at my pre-Sunday hair-combing ritual, "I done seen many a little boy and little girl cry, and your tears don't mean nothing to me. Now, we got to get you pretty for church."

Sidenote for those of you who are only kids: Let me tell you how a younger sibling works. Ten years later, here comes my sister. Grandma is combing her hair, and my sister starts to cry. My grandma turns to my mom and says, "I just can't stand to see Keda cry." Note there was no mention of the number of little children she had seen cry before her, and no mention of whether this changed the validity of the tears of the crying grandchild in front of her.

After several weeks, my grandma grew tired of doing my hair. She'd had it. Enough was enough. My grandma didn't even do her own hair, so she started taking me to her hairdresser, Ms. Martha. My grandma is the type of Southern Black woman who says hairdresser instead of hairstylist, pocketbook instead of purse, and commode instead of toilet. Ms. Martha was a brown-skinned, thick-hipped, cigarette-smoking Black woman. She had her own beauty shop right next door to a barber shop. If you wanted cigarettes, candy, snacks, or a soda, you had to walk over to the barber shop because that's where all the vending machines were.

These were not the days of hairstyle and comfort. Ms. Martha had a shampoo chair that let up a few degrees and let down a few degrees. The rigid black shampoo sink was the height it was without much deference to how that affected you or your neck or your ears or how much water you might get on you. Ms. Martha really could not give attention to such concerns.

The process of the press and curl was fraught with enough neck jerking to count as a chiropractic visit, enough sizzling to make you think you ordered the fajita plate at TGI Fridays, and the satisfied result that if you could sleep like a zombie and avoid all water, moisture, or steam you could be cute for at least two weeks.

Ms. Martha used a hot comb and a set of Marcel irons to perform the signature style of a press and curl. My grandma preferred a tight press and curl, with the end result resembling a roller set. My great-grandma wore what she called a pageboy, where she wore her hair straightened in a side part and then curled under. Ms. Martha styled my hair somewhere in between. To wear my hair "out" was too grown a thing for my age, so Ms. Martha typically straightened my hair and curled it so it could still be worn in ponytails and loose plaits.

Getting your hair straightened was normal, which is why I guess it didn't frighten me at first. But when I look back on it there was a lot to be afraid of. First of all, like many women of her generation, Ms. Martha had hard hands. The type of hands that could wipe a kitchen counter with one swipe, iron flat a bedsheet with two swipes, carry one child on each hip and still whoop with a switch or hang laundry on the line as needed. She tossed my head around in that shampoo bowl like she was about to slide my head down a bowling lane toward a set of bowling pins. I spent the few minutes of hair washing with my shoulders glued to my ears. She twisted my neck every which way to shampoo and then rinsed my hair with no care or concern as to whether my neck was still connected to my head or not.

After my hair was washed and blow-dried, an iron comb was slid into a mini electric oven, an oven so hot that Ms. Martha kept a set of towels, one wet and one dry, to attempt to cool off the hot comb before straightening my hair. Before the hot comb could be applied, she put enough grease on me to make me slide down the street. Then she took the hot comb out of the hot mini stove, sizzled it on the wet towel, dried it off on a dry towel, then the comb sizzled as it slid down my greased-up hair.

Two other pivotal things happened when I would see Ms. Martha. One, we always arrived at a point in the hair-pressing process where she would ask me to hold down my ear. This was expressly so that she could use a *hot iron comb* on the little, teeny, tiny hairs above my ear. Two, if I said ouch when she did this, she would tell me, "Oh, baby, that's just steam." *Narrator voice*: It was never just steam.

During this time, my grandma, Ms. Martha, and the other grown women in the shop talked about grown woman things. It was understood as the child in this situation, I was being given the privilege to hear said conversation, but I was not being given the privilege to be a part of said conversation. They talked about their "stories," which was code for their favorite daytime soap operas. They talked about men, theirs and other people's. They talked about newspaper headlines and little morsels of gossip that had made their way around town.

By the time I thought I couldn't stand it anymore—the heat, the neck discomfort, my butt having lost all feeling from being glued to the chair—Ms. Martha announced I was finished and turned me around to see myself in the mirror. There before me was a new Black girl version of myself. She had shiny, straight hair down to her shoulder blades. She was as close as I would get to looking anything like Brooke Shields. I loved her. She was instantly pretty for church.

The press and curl presented a certain kind of early conflict. I wanted my hair to be easy, to be breezy, to be Pert Plus or whatever, but I also experienced straight hair taking up way more space than I wished it did. The press and curl became this painful beauty experience that gave my mom, my grandma, and me a period of slight unease. I could only hope my hairstyle would hold up as long as I put my hair in some tight shower cap bubble when I showered, didn't sweat, didn't go swimming, didn't get caught in the humidity or in the rain. Which basically meant the press and curl counted for something as long as I existed in a desert or on the surface of Mars.

But on a cloudless Sunday for church, on Easter Sunday against the backdrop of a white dress with white socks with lace paired with black patent leather shoes, on the day of a flawless school picture or a family wedding, family reunion or any other important occasion, the press and curl reigned supreme. Its shiny, lacquered curls and straightness told the world your mother, your grandmother, your aunt, or whatever adult woman you were with cared about you. You became an excellent reflection of their class and decorum. It didn't matter if you weren't allowed to play rough and tumble with other kids. It didn't matter if you stared longingly at the little boys your age with their barber shop haircuts running around after church or at a family gathering, wishing you too could play freeze tag. You would catch the eye of whichever Black woman was responsible for your flawless press and curl and think better of it.

The first sight of a new press and curl provided a momentary anesthesia and amnesia. All of a sudden, I wasn't worried about that "steam" that left a mark on my ear or my sore neck from the shampoo bowl. All I could do was feel pretty. At least until it rained or got really humid, or until I wanted to go to the pool. Then, it was back to Ms. Martha's.

STRAIGHT HAIR, DON'T CARE

don't get my hair pressed anymore. This is a *perm*," one of my fifth-grade classmates said.

We gathered around her, studying her edges and the movability of her ponytail. We murmured among ourselves during another straight hair evangelist's sermon, "What is a perm?" She didn't know how to explain it, except to tell us somebody put some creamy stuff on her hair and now she didn't have to worry about the rain ruining her hair or any accusations of being tenderheaded. She ran her fingers through her hair as proof.

When I got home from school and watched what little TV I was allowed, it felt like a perm was calling me. Between the PCJ no-lye perm commercials exclaiming I could be PCJoyful and PCJumpin' and PCJazzy, and the Just for Me! perm commercials with their catchy jingle and spelling lesson, J–U–S–T–F–O–R–M–E, I was convinced the perm was for me! Since I was headed into middle school, my mom didn't take too much convincing. The commercials were promising a better life to Black moms and daughters, with less ouch, so they said. But the perm didn't mean the process was without pain.

A hairstylist would grease my edges and scalp, mix the chemicals for the perm—which later came to be called a relaxer, even though nothing about the process was relaxing—and apply this creamy chemical concoction to my roots, only to let it sit while it "relaxed" my tight curls. The first few minutes were kind of relaxing. I was a middle school student sitting in the swirl of some of the best conversations between Black women I'd ever hear. I could get in people's business. I could investigate the mobile vendors that inevitably walked through the salon selling wares from jewelry to food to maintenance services. Laughter would ensue, until I noticed my scalp was starting to burn a little.

At first, I'm not even sure it could be characterized as a burn. At first it was a tingle? My hairstylist would come back and check on me, pop gum, brush my hair lightly with the same brush she used to install the perm to see "did the perm take?" and inevitably draw the conclusion that my hair had not relaxed enough yet. And here is typically where the hairstylist and I would have a standoff.

The tingle would steadily increase to a burn. It started in the back or on the edges and would spread like . . . wildfire . . . please accept these similes . . . throughout my whole head. I was starting to feel like this was an emergency, like maybe the fire department needed to be called? Could there be a mini fire department that specialized in these types of fires?! My hair and scalp needed to go to the emergency room, and could I meet them there?!

I'd speak up. My hairstylist would pop her gum and eyeball me. She knew the relaxer wasn't ready. The perm needed more time to "take." Her option was to convince me I could wait, or she'd succumb to my urgent pleading, wash out this perm with uneven kinky and straight results, and be forced to fix it again later.

The hairstylists in this situation had great negotiating tactics. I was a client out on the ledge of perm pain, ready to jump into "maybe I just don't need hair at all." The stylist would remind me of things I'd like to be pretty for (church, school, a family gathering, a school dance). They would then describe what the situation could be if I didn't endure this pain. Maybe my hair would fall out. Maybe my hair would be half done. Maybe I'd be embarrassed—as a middle school student who had already been bullied, this was probably the most effective method. I couldn't do anything about my skinny legs or my long feet or my four eyes because of my glasses, but I could do something about whether or not I gave this perm enough time to "take."

So sometimes I'd wait another eternity. Now no jokes were funny. No snack could be offered to assuage me. I was watching the second hand of the salon clock as if I could time my own relief. As if my life depended on it, because my scalp depended on it. A pop of gum and a perm check were completed. Sometimes a compromise was had. My hairstylist would say we can wash out the back and I would follow her to the shampoo bowl as if my scalp were a parched desert survivor who had just arrived at its first canteen of water.

This would bring some relief, but even washing out the back made me feel as if needle points were being broken off and carried away as the perm disappeared into the sink. Then I'd have another clockless, humorless wait for the front of my hair to "take" before I would at last be permitted for the whole of the perm to be washed out. Alas shampoo, conditioner, relief!

From here, there was setting lotion, time under the dryer, side part, layers of curls, and the glorious vision of straight-haired me who would remain this way for six to eight weeks before I had to return to the salon. That future self would sometimes go home and nurse chemical scalp burns and irritation. But I didn't take much time to think about that. I was too busy focusing on how cute I felt, albeit semi-permanently.

By the time I was twelve I was styling my own relaxed hair. This was the early 1990s and this was a time for Black girl hair and relaxers. This was the era of the French roll, fingerwaves, the high ponytail, stiff cascading bangs, the wrap, the wash and set, the roller set. This was an era of crunchy hairstyles, where if you slept like a mummy, they could last for weeks. Questions could be asked as to whether they *should* have lasted for weeks, but that's for another chapter.

My products of choice had changed. It was all about Ampro Pro Styl gel. How was I supposed to get all this hair on the top of my head *and* arrange it into a cascade of curls?! How was I supposed to turn my sideburns into lightning bolts?

The high ponytail was my favorite style. I owned three curling irons of various sizes that helped me achieve my cascade bangs and curly ponytail. When I wasn't wearing my high ponytail, complete with hoodie, Starter jacket, and gold hoops, I wore my hair down, slightly curled on the ends.

Sometime in high school my hair started breaking off. This is also a common Black girl story. We know more now about how to achieve amazing styles without sacrificing the integrity of the hair—but back then? Style was king! Look at these fingerwaves! We can think of hair health later!

By this time, I had my own hairstylist. She was much younger and closer in age to me and was the first one to tell me that my hair was breaking off and the only way forward required a haircut. I was never interested in a haircut. I was still striving for that long, luxurious hair I'd seen white women, and some Black women, have, but when she showed me that the hair at the crown of my head had decided to break up with me without letting me know in advance, I agreed to the cut.

She cut me a shag with more length on top, tapered sides and tapered in the back leading into a row of flip curls. When she showed me my new hair with layers of curls, shiny and stiff, I felt like I looked cute but *Whitney Houston voice* *How would I know?!* School wasn't the true test, and neither were my friends. The true test was the mall.

Ah, the mall. In historic eras past, the mall was a very important building for a young American teenager. I'll explain for anyone who has only heard the term *mall* in a sociology or archaeology class. The mall was a large building filled with many stores, kiosks, and a massive food court. There were anchor stores where you typically went with your parents when you weren't with your friends and where you hoped your friends wouldn't see you with your parents. Your mom might take you to Sears or JCPenney to go clothes shopping. Your grandma might want to just do a quick walkthrough of Ward's or Belk's, neither of which had an *s* in their name at all. These were not stores you walked through with your friends.

Trips to the mall had to be coordinated and negotiated among friends. In a time of no texting and no cell phones, all plans were solidified in person or on the landline at your parents' house. This meant, depending on the type of Black household you came from, your friends' mall logistics call could be interrupted by a mom who would pick up the other landline phone and without apologizing for the interruption or saying "Excuse me" or saying "Hey, kids, how y'all doing?" would announce, "I need to use the phone."

Three things had to be considered in planning a mall trip in high school. Here is where you choose your own adventure. First, how will you get there? Do you have your license? Does your friend have a license? Are either of you permitted to drive other teenagers around with that license? If this doesn't work, does one of you have an older sibling that your parents trust to drive you and your friends to the mall? Do you have an older sibling that you trust to drive you to the mall without embarrassing you? If this is an option, go with this. You will experience some leniency this way. Last resort is if none of these options work and you have to ask a parent. Does one of you have a "cool" parent? A Kool-Aid parent? A parent that will ask the bare minimum of questions and not insist on being seen with you at the mall? If this doesn't work, take the parent who is available. Being embarrassed by your parent is a travesty but not being able to go to the mall when all your friends are there is much, much worse.

Once you have secured your ride to the mall, your next factor to consider is time. You don't want to get to the mall too early. It is clear to you as a teenager that people over thirty years old want to go to the mall closer to when it opens, do their shopping, grab lunch, and be home before three p.m. This is not the case for a teenager mall trip in the 1990s. There is a mall sweet spot. The goody-two-shoes kids arrive around lunchtime because that's when their very attentive parents drop them off. Then there's the second wave of kids who have an older sibling or can drive themselves. They arrive around two p.m. with plans to stay at least until five or six. Then there's the third wave, the people who have parents or guardians who are not watching over them closely, who see no problem with teenagers leaving the house around four and staying until the mall closes. Your mall sweet spot was to be at the mall when all three waves of people were present.

This meant you had to negotiate a drop-off and pickup time that would not ruin your fun. This was easier to negotiate with an older sibling, but an attentive parent? Much harder to influence. Attentive parents want to know things like, "Who all gon' be there? What you gon' be doing besides walking around the mall? With whose money? You ain't got mall money." But if you could assuage the attentive parent's concern, convince them that you wanted to get to the mall around three or four p.m. and seven or eight p.m. would be great for pickup time, you were well on your way to having a great time stuntin' at the local mall.

The mall was the true test of my new haircut. My friends and I were gonna run into people we went to school with and by people I really mean BOYS. Boys dressed in Tommy Hilfiger and FILA. BOYS wearing way too much Cool Water cologne. Black boys who wore durags so tight you thought they'd lose circulation in their face, just so they could showcase their flawless waves.

My friends, my new haircut, and I arrived at the mall. We went to the food court because somebody always wanted an Auntie Anne's pretzel or an Orange Julius. We'd do our first lap, walking into stores we liked. We perused the mall music store to see what CDs were for sale and to look at the cool posters they had of artists in there. We stopped through Hot Topic and Spencer's because one of us was always secretly a little goth and because both stores had items for sale that had sex jokes and turns of phrase we somehow wanted to be thought of as mature enough to be able to see but were still immature enough that these things made us giggle. We stopped through Foot Locker to stare at the latest sneakers, and then we'd head back to the food court.

Inevitably, one of us had arranged a clandestine meeting with someone our parents had no idea we had a crush on, our friends agreeing to hide this intention. So that day, as we were sitting in the food court, waiting on my friend's crush to arrive, it happened. The finest group of the finest Black boys in my school were walking toward us. Wearing brown and red and white and blue, their brown skin dressed in coordinating Tommy Hilfiger that might as well have been kings' robes to me. I was friends with one of them because we went to church together. He is the reason they stopped to speak. I'm sure they walked up to us regular but to me they had created their own music video. They were walking toward us to the rhythm of the Fugees' "Ready or Not" and I wasn't sure I was ready or not, but I stood to greet them.

"Got your hair cut?" Calvin, my secret crush, said.

"I like it. It looks good," Greg said.

If it's possible for one's whole being to smile, that's what my whole being did that day. Growing up, I never felt like a pretty girl, but that day Calvin and Greg made me wonder if I'd been a pretty girl all along.

I wore my hair in this very haircut until I left home to attend Spelman College. Leaving home to go to college is exciting and scary. You are leaving your family and watching your friends scatter to their own post–high school plans. When I arrived on campus I had one urgent concern: I needed to find a hairstylist. I studied the hair of the upperclasswomen and asked some of them for hairstylist recommendations, but many of them lived off campus or went to get their hair done somewhere you could only drive to, and since I didn't have a car my first year of school, that wasn't an option. Thankfully, there was a small strip of shops across the street from campus and there was a Black salon there called Mass Appeal. I made an appointment and a hairstylist named April with a shiny gold tooth became my college hairstylist.

My first year of Spelman we took a class called African Diaspora and the World, which felt like a crash course boot camp of all of the Black history we had not been taught in school. We read Chinua Achebe and Beverly Guy-Sheftall. We read about systems of oppression, hierarchies of oppression, about feminism and womanism, about assimilation and white supremacy. This course, alongside our other classes, radicalized many of my Spelman siblings. Classmates who started out at Spelman with long, relaxed hair and cute, pixie straight cuts began growing their perms out, and when their hair grew long enough, they cut off the permed ends and wore tiny afros. I gave them the Black power fist, and I also continued my standing appointment with April every six weeks for a touch-up.

By the time we reached our junior year, many of my classmates wore afros and locs and twists and braids. A couple of them, now natural hair evangelists, pulled me to the side to discuss my hair's soul.

"Amena, after all you've learned, you still want to stay committed to the creamy crack?" they'd say.

I would look at their hair in the in-between stage of growing out and nod my head yes. If getting a perm was wrong, I didn't want to be right. By senior year, they tried to appeal to my intelligence, to my respect for science.

"Amena, did you know that perm residue stays on your scalp for the rest of your life? When you die you could still have a layer of perm sitting on your brain?"

I touched their shoulders to let them know I appreciated their concern and reminded them we all have to go someday and when I go, I'd like my hair to be fried, dyed, and laid to the side. They walked away muttering prayers for my heathen scalp and soul.

By the time we graduated from college my natural hair Spelman siblings' awkward afros had grown into luxurious locs, beautiful bald heads, and conscious curls. My permed hair that I was very proud of had grown down to my shoulders. Many of us transitioned into grad school and corporate jobs in the early 2000s, trying to discern if the world of business or academics welcomed us and our hair. Many of my Spelman siblings rebelled against the narrow norms of the spaces in which they found themselves, daring to wear their hair in whichever way they wanted. Some of my Spelman siblings hoped their straight hair would help them climb whichever corporate ladder they'd chosen. I just wanted my hair to blow in the wind like Sanaa Lathan's hair in *Brown Sugar*.

I transitioned to an early 2000s Halle Berry cut and wore this into my mid-twenties. I wore it slicked down. I wore it curled. I wore it spiked. In the six to eight weeks between perm touch-ups I loved my straight hair but I never grew to love the process, I just endured it. I learned to fear my new growth and the times I had to wait longer to straighten my hair than I wanted to. I wore my straight hair strong until I went broke and could no longer afford a relaxer.

LETTER TO MY HAIR

I first noticed you when I was about three
My friend's mom carved and twisted you into rows
Punctuated with tinfoil and beads
That was the first time I learned you could swing
I loved you then

Until Grandma tried to get me pretty for church
And you would not cooperate
So we greased you up
Branded you with a hot iron comb
You fought and hissed and finally submitted
You lay down
Decided to bend and curl as we instructed you

I felt sorry for you
And maybe you felt sorry for me too

For tips of ears and back of neck sacrificed
For innocent hairs singed

For pain tolerance learned
For curling iron forehead scars
For holding down my ear for fear I'd be burned

School started and I began to resent you
Back then
High side ponytails were in
I wanted you to behave the same as the strands of Tiffany
    and Debbie Gibson
I realized I was neither brunette nor blond
You had no intentions of going along with this

I was angry with you
Pinned you down
Held you tight
Tied you up
Until I hurt both of us

I cried
Because I was pretty sure I hated you
It seemed you were never what I wanted you to be
You would not lie
Only stand
You would not blow in the wind
Only lean against it
So I decided to get you fixed

For twenty years
I subjected you to concoctions

I hoped would teach you not to be yourself
To convince you for the rest of my life to be like someone else
I hoped to teach you to be yourself isn't okay
Isn't enough
To remind you there is a norm and you need to conform
So you did

Until I noticed you
Trying to push past who I'd made you into
For the first time in a long time
I realized I had wronged you
Maybe it was time to let you be
I remembered you were beautiful
I cut you loose
Let you grow
Learned your frequency
You didn't want to be hurt, burned, subjected
You wanted to be free

You wanted to teach me how to love
Because learning to love my curls
Would help me to love my bare face, brown skin, and
    round curves
Would help me to heal the kind of hurt a grown woman
    carries from being a little girl

Loving you is teaching me to love that little girl
And the grown woman she grew up to be
I'm watching you grow
And as you grow, I do too
You remind me every day
We are both beautiful

DOES BEING NATURAL MAKE ME A NUBIAN QUEEN?

went natural in the late aughts. (Wait is that how we describe the late part of the era between 2000 and 2010?!) I didn't go natural because my Spelman classmates had finally proselytized and evangelized my heathen hair and soul. I didn't go natural because I wanted to make any sort of strong political statement. I just went broke.

Yes, Black women change our hair when our life is in a time of transition or transformation. Sometimes the hair change is inspired by a life change. But sometimes the hair change can inspire a life change. This was the case with me.

The level of brokeness I experienced caused me to slowly start removing luxuries from my budget. First, manicures and pedicures. Then eating out with friends. Then concerts and movies. Then hair appointments. I thought I was delaying the hair appointments, not deleting. I had gone so long without getting a perm that my new growth was starting to grow into curls.

Usually, the presence of new growth was a red alert, an urgent alarm that it was time to get my hair done and in a hurry! The feeling of my tight coils next to the straight and smooth relaxed hair felt like an offense to my fingers at first. It had been so long since I'd seen that much of my hair without a relaxer, and the alarm at first was quieter and then it wasn't there at all. The curls at my roots started to feel cool and interesting and curious. What if I could go natural?

I had quit my corporate job to become a writer and poetry performer full-time, but the contracts and gigs were coming in slowly and sometimes not at all. When money trickled in, I had to downgrade from my regular high-end hairstylist to a salon that ran a special on $40 relaxers. I decided to confess to this hairstylist stranger that I was considering going natural, like you'd confess to your doctor you're thinking about becoming pescatarian. Maybe a professional hairstylist would give me things to think about, helpful tips for transitioning out of my relaxer like a doctor might encourage me to make sure I still get certain nutrients as I change my diet.

Because my relaxed hair was already short, my new growth was showing itself much more in the back than anywhere else. My temporary hairstylist draped me with a black plastic cape and started the process of putting grease on my edges to prepare me for my relaxer.

"I'm thinking about going natural," I said.

"Really?" she said.

"Yes," I said.

She took the skinny end of her rat tail comb and pointed it at the back of my hair.

"You want your whole head to look like this?!" she said.

The rest of the appointment was in silence. I walked out

with my re-relaxed hair, but I had never felt so dissatisfied with it. I got one more $40 perm a couple of months later and decided it would be my last. Between these two perms, I decided not to renew the lease on my apartment because I could no longer afford the rent. A friend of a friend offered me a room and a bathroom to rent and I was also going through a breakup. My hair and I were both down bad.

I felt like a failure because I went through a breakup and went broke at the same time. I didn't have enough income as a writer and performer, so I started working a customer service job on the phones. By now my hair had grown beyond my hair care expertise. I knew how to shampoo and condition my hair. I knew how to blow-dry and use my curling irons, but the last time I'd seen my natural hair I was wearing pigtails. I had no idea what to do with my returned texture. I needed a professional.

I found a salon that specialized in curly hair and natural hair and made an appointment there. I was assigned a beautiful Black woman named Giselle to style my hair that day. By the time I arrived in her chair, I had a tiny afro in the back of my hair and some strong strands of straight hair hanging on for dear life in the front.

Giselle did an assessment of my hair and she said, "You're gonna have to make a decision today. Either we have to cut your remaining relaxed hair today and you're going to walk out of here with just your natural hair. Or you could get braids, a weave, or some other protective style and let your hair grow out a little bit longer so your hair is longer when you cut it."

At that time, I hadn't had braids in years and my scalp normally didn't handle them well anyway. I'd never had a weave and wasn't sure I'd be able to afford one, so I told her I was ready to cut it that day.

I didn't know this was called a Big Chop at the time. She

cut my hair, and it was probably an inch long all around. She dyed my hair a firecracker red. I'd never had my hair dyed before either. When Giselle turned me around to face the mirror at her styling station, I wasn't sure what to expect, but I liked the beautiful face, eyes, and red curly afro in front of me. It was more of my face than I'd seen in years, but I felt beautiful and triumphant. Giselle told me what products to get to take care of my hair and I walked out of the salon with new products, new hair, and what felt like a renewed sense of confidence.

I left the hair salon and went straight to work at my phone customer service job for the evening shift. I had a coworker who sat next to me, and we were used to talking to each other while the other person was face forward typing up notes from finishing a call. She had already launched into a story about her day when she turned and noticed my hair. She gasped.

"What happened?!" she said, aghast with her hand on her chest.

"I cut my hair," I said.

"Yeah, I see that. But why?! Why would you do that?!"

I didn't have a good answer. I also hadn't contemplated that other people might not think my new natural hair looked good on me. It was dawning on me I had made what at the time seemed like a perfectly reasonable and possibly amazing decision, but now felt reckless and really permanent.

Sidenote: Do not make drastic changes to your hair and then go straight to work if you can help it. Give yourself some private time to adjust. This will save you a lot of uncomfortable feelings in the future.

I took my short lunch break, scarfing down my food quickly so I could spend the rest of my break calling friends who could be my lifeline as if I was on a natural-hair-themed episode of *Who Wants to Be a Millionaire?* called *Who Wants to Go Natural?* My first lifeline was my college friend Asha. In college she had worn her hair in all these amazing braided natural hairstyles, so I figured she'd know what to do, she'd know what to tell me, she'd be able to convince me I hadn't just made a big mistake.

"You didn't make the wrong decision," she said. "You made the right decision, but you're going to have to be patient and learn how to take care of your hair."

Despite my coworker's reaction, Asha's encouraging words helped carry me through my shift. The next morning, I realized I had a social event to go to. I woke up and freaked out. I called my next hair lifeline, one of my best friends, Adrienne.

"Go to YouTube and put 'natural hair' in the search. All these videos are going to pull up and that'll give you some suggestions on what to do," she said.

I thought that was the silliest thing she ever told me because I didn't know a lot about YouTube at the time. This was the late aughts, remember?! Why would I go to a place that has cat videos to find videos of natural hair stuff?! But I did what she said because I woke up in the middle of the next night feeling super anxious about this choice I'd made. My "natural hair" YouTube search pulled up all these helpful videos.

Solange had just cut her hair short, and she was doing these cool parts in her hair with bejeweled accessories. I was able to see an example of someone whose hair was closer to the length and texture I had. I was able to see Black women taking pictures and video of themselves getting their Big Chop, taking pictures of their hair growing over time so I could see that, even though I may have been feeling nervous then, in six months, in a year, I could possibly look at my hair and have a fuller afro.

I went natural a few months before my thirtieth birthday. I learned my natural curl pattern, the way my roots grew in, the different parts of my hair that had different curl patterns. I was learning how to take care of my hair and style my hair.

I was learning to be gentle with myself and my hair. These are lessons I'm still learning. My natural hair journey has been a beautiful journey for me. Wearing my braids or my natural hair has been the best thing for me and the best thing for my hair.

Black women deserve the freedom to wear our hair as it naturally grows out of our scalps, to let our hair grow out and take up space and be big and unruly if it wants to, while finding the freedom in that. Black women can do our hair however we want to. A Black woman can have no hair or a smooth fade. She can have a wig or a weave. She can have braids or a relaxer. She can wear an afro or locs. She can do whatever she wants to with her hair, her body, herself.

Black women, wear your hair however you want to. Wear it big. Wear it long. Wear it straight. Wear it curly. Wear different wigs every day. There are so many ways to Black Girl, which means the way you Black Girl is beautiful, and the way I Black Girl is beautiful too.

BOX BRAIDS AND THE ANNUAL BLACK GIRL MEETING

When I was a little girl, ours was not a hair do-it-yourself house. My mom believed four things required a hair professional: cut, color, chemicals, and braids. Like Indigo in Spike Lee's movie *Mo' Better Blues*, my mom wore a tapered cut with her curls slightly texturized. For her own hair, she depended on the expertise of her hairstylist, Norris, for haircuts and any chemical hair treatments. When my mom wore her hair in braided styles, she had the convenience of having found an excellent braider in our apartment building. To slow down what my mom figured would be my eventual journey toward a relaxer, she set me up with her braider to get my hair braided with extensions when I was in elementary school. This gave both of us a rest from "Ow!" and "Be still!" and "Tenderheaded."

The first couple of weeks with my new braids were exhilarating. I could pull them back in a ponytail or fasten them up with a bow. I could run and play, and my mom would be less concerned with how my hair would survive. But the next couple of weeks an itchy, flaky scalp would surface. My scalp itched so bad, I wanted to take off my scalp and trade it in for a new one. There was no such thing then as a curl custard or a twist out smoothie or a coily pudding. My scalp only had two options: Pink Oil Moisturizer and Blue Magic hair grease. Neither of which was really going to help my itchy scalp at all. This means the 1980s was the last time I wore box braids.

After being natural for several years, I had learned how to finger coil, how to wash and go, how to twist and how to twist out. I accepted my free-range curls, how they would grow big and rowdy in the humid summer, tighter and in need of more moisture in the winter. I longed for my twist out to transform into a beautiful afro; I loved the unpredictability of my hair. I learned how to style an amazing twist out before an event or a performance, learned to retwist if my hair had to be consistent for a multi-day event or video shoot. All of this was fine, great, acceptable, until I was invited to be onstage at Essence Festival, also referred to by me as The Annual Black Girl Meeting. This was going to be my first time at Essence Fest, and I was hosting game shows on the Beauty Carnival Stage. I could not look or be basic. I could not leave my hair to chance.

I called around to all my girlfriends who had been to Essence Fest. I consulted my hairstylist and a personal stylist. The conclusion was that my twist out and my afro would not survive the drenching New Orleans heat for multiple days. I would end up retwisting my hair every night to be stage-ready only for my cute twist out to possibly morph into a lopsided afro on the walk from my hotel to the exhibit hall. Almost every Black woman I talked to recommended I get box braids.

I immediately got nervous. I didn't have a braider on standby. The few recommendations I could get either were booked months out or were not for novices or re-novices like me. My Black women friends were used to this. They had their own braiding routines. I had way more questions than answers. This mission would require meticulous research and prompt investigation.

With the same precision Nev and Kamie would use to suss out a catfish, I began my search for a braider who I could verify had the styles, skills, and expertise to handle a re-beginner like me. I started with Google, cross-referenced the results with Yelp, then narrowed down the braiding salons based on their Instagram feeds. I scheduled my appointment, and paid extra for the wash and blow-dry, because all my tries at blow-drying my own hair had resulted in a huge helmet of hair that did not want to be this way. According to the instructions of the braiding salon, I needed to bring four packs of a specified brand of braiding hair to my appointment. I gulped. Now this mission would require a trip to the beauty supply store!

When my mom first started getting my hair braided when I was a little girl, a braid appointment included the braider providing the hair. I remember my mom going to the salon to get her hair braided and the braider walking next door to the beauty supply to buy the hair, a snack, and possibly a pack of smokes. I learned quickly those days were done!

I live in one of the Blackest cities in America and although the number of Black-owned beauty supplies has increased, the number is still very few. Venturing into a non-Black-owned beauty supply can mean you may experience a few things. You could be followed as you search for your items. You could have questions about a product when it comes to your particular hair or skin tone, and the people working there may not be able to answer the questions. The cashier may not look you in the eyes at any time during the transaction. The store itself may present an environment that says we want your money but not you.

I try as much as I can to shop at Black-owned beauty supply stores, because there is something fulfilling about going to a place for a product where the people who work there know what you're using it for and how to answer your questions. So, I drove out of my way, out of my neighborhood to a different side of town to support a Black-owned beauty supply store and to let them support me as I realized on the way over how much I had no idea what the hell I was doing.

I walked into a well-organized, bright retail space and asked the Black woman at the counter where I could find braiding hair. She looked at my hair color and suggested a color she thought matched and left me to consider my decisions in the aisle. There were one-packs. There were three-packs. There were all sorts of colors and lengths. There was ombre. I was confused trying to decide between them.

I went back to the email confirmation for my braiding appointment and saw a number to call if I had any questions. I called it out of desperation and a Black woman picked up the phone, who I later found out was the owner of the salon. I said something I'm sure was a full sentence but in my head sounded like "braids . . . color . . . how long . . . packs?" She talked me through, and I walked out with eight packs of hair in two different colorways because I prefer to be overprepared, and I didn't want to be Black Salon Embarrassed.

When I got home, I went to YouTube, which for better or for worse is its own Black Woman Hair University. The YouTube girlies told me to soak my braiding hair in apple cider vinegar mixed with water to remove the outer coating of the hair that may cause those with sensitive scalps to be itchy. Could this be the reason my scalp was so itchy with braids as a child?!

I did as the YouTube natural hair girlies instructed and made a vinegar soaking bath for my braiding hair: soaking, rinsing, gently squeezing until damp, then looping each hair pack onto a clothes hanger to dry.

The day of my appointment I took my nervous ass and way too many packs of braiding hair to the salon. I met my braider, who I knew had to be a grown woman but looked like she had somehow escaped from high school to braid hair in her spare time.

I laid my head in the shampoo bowl as I'd done hundreds of times before. She washed and blow-dried my hair way more quickly than it would have gone had I done it, and while she braided my hair, I observed the usual goings-on in a Black hair salon. The customer complaining about the price. The hairstylist with relationship problems. The random movie on the TV that I otherwise would not have watched. When my braider finished the braids, she came back to the chair with a pitcher of hot water.

"What are you going to do with that?" I asked, thinking it was a bit late in the appointment to offer tea.

"Seal your braids at the end," she said.

"You can do that with water?" I said.

She looked at me and gave me a small smile as if to say she felt sorry for my basic ass.

"When I was little, they used to seal the braids with a lighter," I said.

"Oh yeah, I remember my mom doing that," she said.

And there's nothing like someone insinuating you are the same age or generation as their mother.

I walked out with large box braids down to my bra strap, and when I looked at myself in the mirror, I had transformed into an amazing Nubian queen. I swung my hair as I had so many times after various salon appointments. For the next several weeks, I would be *insufferable*. I had summoned the energy of Beyoncé's braids hanging out of the El Camino in the "Formation" video, of Janet Jackson's box braids in *Poetic Justice* when she told Tupac "I'm a Black woman, okay? I deserve respect!," of Brandy's braids cascading on her bed when she was sitting up in her room. I was transfixed and transformed. I joined the collective of summer braids Black women.

My time at Essence Festival was a busy blur of sweaty walks down New Orleans streets, amazing New Orleans food, and so many Black women living their best lives. The Essence Festival theme that year was "It's the Black Joy for Me." Yes, Essence, for me too.

The flight from Atlanta to New Orleans might as well have been a Black chartered plane. It would have been fitting if the flight attendants had played "Before I Let Go" (both Beyoncé's and Frankie Beverly's versions) and the electric slide had broken out in the aisle. I joined the ranks of so many Black women on the flight—who had also preemptively gotten their hair braided for this trip—and we were headed to an event that had colloquially become an Auntie Mecca. I questioned if I had fully transitioned to being an auntie, but I definitely wanted my pilgrimage.

I arrived in New Orleans a day before the festival began and every Black-owned restaurant and shop within a five-mile radius of the Superdome was already packed! I planned outfits to walk over to the exhibit hall in and carried my outfits for hosting. Several Black women hair and makeup artists were at the ready to touch up those of us who were speaking or performing onstage. During the day I hosted game shows featuring celebrities and influencers. I hosted a game show featuring the Silver Fox Squad, a crew of several men of the salt-and-pepper-beard age, and I have never seen so many Black women of all ages lose their ability to breathe air for a few minutes.

The Silver Fox Squad filled the backstage area with the scent of expensive cologne; the kind of cologne that made you feel like it wrapped its arms around you and held you for a few minutes. As a married woman of over a decade I had to remind myself I was indeed going home to my fine husband and not one of these silver foxy fine men. I had a home. I would return there. I repeated this to myself until their segment was over.

At night, when I was done working, I had time to enjoy the evening concerts featuring the Fugees, Chloe x Halle, Summer Walker, Jazmine Sullivan, Patti LaBelle, City Girls (before they broke up), Lil' Kim, The Roots & Friends, and New Edition. The artist I was most excited to see was Janet Jackson. I have loved Janet since I was wearing box braids as a child. I put her posters on my wall. I sent a letter with one of my school pictures to her fan club. It was basically a snail mail version of a fan DM.

As Janet put on a show for the ages, as I sang to "Rhythm Nation" and "The Pleasure Principle" and "Control" and "Escapade," I swung myself and my braids from side to side. Little Mena would be so proud of me, wearing braids with no scalp itch and no lighters, watching one of my favorite artists do her thing onstage, singing and rapping along with an arena full of Black women getting their life and getting their joy. She would be so proud of how beautiful it still is to be a Black girl.

Braids have so many cultural layers for us as Black American women. They are a style our mothers, aunties, grandmothers arranged for us to ease our lives and theirs. Braids connect us back to the parts of our African ancestry that were stolen from us. They help us ease our way into the pool, the ocean, a stage, a photo shoot, a wedding, without worry about how our hair may evolve with a bit of extra sun or water.

Braids are also complicated. Many Black women for years felt they couldn't wear braids in the workplace because they were seen as unkempt or unprofessional. Famous white women adorned their hair with braids and tried to rename them boxer braids, attempting to erase all the innovating Black women have done with braids across the diaspora.

I thought of this as I walked the streets of New Orleans and did the electric slide with thousands of other Black women on what has become an annual pilgrimage to celebrate Black joy, Black music, and Black heritage. I thought about how beautiful we are in all our shades and shapes. How expressive we are from our hair to our eyebrows, our fingernails to our lipstick. I smiled and tossed my braids over my shoulder. I love us.

SEVEN WAYS YOU CAN BE BLACK SALON EMBARRASSED

f I close my eyes and think about a Black hair salon, I can still smell the combination of chemicals, shampoo, and smoke (from the Marcel irons and from a hairstylist's recent smoke break). I can hear variations of "Girl!" and "Uh uh!" and "I know she didn't!"

There are a few places that hold a certain kind of shared Black cultural memory. One of them is the Black church, but there are many other temples of Black culture, and the Black hair salon is one of them. These experiences have been chronicled in films such as *Beauty Shop, Nappily Ever After,* and *School Daze.* There is muscle memory to the Black salon. How you enter. How you exit. Who you might encounter there.

Today, there are salon suites, a typically quiet, quaint experience where you have your hair appointment with just you and your hairstylist, but for most of my life this was not the case. Most of my Black salon experiences were a combination of standup comedy, lessons in good and bad customer service, good and bad customers, political commentary, roundtable relationship discussions, and performance art. There were regulars who typically got their hair done on a system of clocked-in consistent appointments. There were new clients who had no idea what they were walking into. There were little girls having their first of what would be many hair appointments.

There were the seasoned hairstylists who'd been doing hair for twenty years or more and felt a French roll and fingerwaves were proper for any occasion. The young hairstylists who kept up with hair trends and tried new products, new styles, new color techniques. The shampoo assistant who was still in beauty school and wanted to learn as much as possible from the other stylists but couldn't be trusted beyond applying conditioner and was not allowed to get too close to certain clients for fear the shampoo assistant could steal them away.

One thing no one wanted to experience was Black Salon Embarrassment, a phenomenon that could result in distress, difficulty, or feelings of awkwardness or shame. This could occur because of the state of a client's hair when they walked in or the state of their hair when they walked out. This could occur because of the state of a client's attitude when they walked in or the state of their attitude when they walked out. This could occur because of the external factors everyone knew about the life of the client or hairstylist, if someone they were sleeping with showed up to the salon, if someone they were dating paid for their hair appointment, if someone they weren't supposed to be sleeping with popped up unannounced.

I attempted to avoid being Black Salon Embarrassed at all costs, by being quiet, keeping to myself, lightly chuckling but not loudly guffawing at anything, by making sure my hair was not in complete shambles when I arrived and being sure to follow general Black rules of greetings, pleases, thank-yous, and yes ma'ams where required.

Many Black salons had some sort of bell attached to the door. The ringing of this bell is how you knew if a previous scene was ending, or a new scene was beginning. If the bell ringing announced a client was leaving, everyone was given permission to talk about said client as soon as the bell rang, signaling the door had closed behind them. As a new client, the ringing of the bell signaled that the door had closed behind you, and you were in new territory.

HERE ARE SOME THINGS YOU CAN DO TO AVOID BEING BLACK SALON EMBARRASSED

1. Bring Greetings

There are many Black communal moments where the right thing to do, the first thing to start with, is speaking. In many Black churches, visitors bring greetings, announcing where they are from, if they belong to a church there, who the pastor is, what their testimony is, and how you can pray for them.

The script of greeting goes something like this:

"Giving honor to God" or "Give an honor to God who is the head of my life.

"I bring you greetings from [insert church name here], where my pastor is the [insert lofty adjectives here, e.g., most righteous, most eloquent, most auspicious] [insert title here: Bishop, Rev., Dr., etc.] [pastor's government name].

"Today I want to thank God for [choose from options below]:

- My health and strength
- Grace and mercy
- The fact that my bed wasn't my cooling board

[Leave room for congregational praise here]
"Please pray for [insert prayer requests]:

- My family
- The sick and shut in

"And please continue to pray my strength. Amen."

After this, the congregation feels properly greeted and spoken to and the new visitor is welcomed into the church community.

In many Black cookouts, holidays, and family functions, children and adults alike are expected to speak and greet when they first walk into a home. It is necessary to greet anyone you see in any room you walk into and it is especially pertinent to greet the host and whoever's home it is. This could amount to seventy-two hellos and thirty-eight how you doin's, but each hello and how you doin' will be said until you have spoken to everyone.

I live in the South, in a Black neighborhood, and many of my neighbors are older Black folks. Whether I am on the phone or huffing and puffing through a workout, a "hi, how you doin'," is expected. A "shole is hot out here" or an "all right now," is possible. We know the white people in our neighborhood who got some sense based on if they speak when we say hello to them.

It is a colossal social faux pax to enter many Black spaces without bringing greetings, head nods, handwaves, hugs, or dap. This is also true in a Black hair salon. And God bless the Black introverts. Despite my current career as a stage performer, I was not a ham growing up. I was a shy, withdrawn, nerdy reader. I was trained over many childhood moves and new schools to learn how to converse with just about anyone about just about anything. But young me? She was quiet and really intimidated at what the speaking expectations were of me, especially if I was entering a Black salon for the first time.

Sometimes there was a receptionist or shampoo assistant, sometimes the first one or two stylists in the stations closest to the door played greeter. You'd engage the receptionist in a quiet conversation where you confirmed your name, the service you booked, and the name of the hairstylist you'd scheduled with. Sometimes the receptionist would point out your new stylist, so you'd have an idea who to look for. But if there was no receptionist, you had to be ready to project from the diaphragm.

A stylist who was busy popping gum and clicking Marcel irons while talking shit to the current client in their chair would look up at you standing near the door, looking forlorn, and say, "Who you here to see, baby?" Heaven help you if you couldn't remember the hairstylist's name.

"Nikki?" you'd say.

"Oh, we ain't got no Nikki here," they'd say.

Then your brain would go blank. This was before Instagram or any social media, so you just had a name someone had said to you on the phone. You didn't have a face to confirm.

"You probably talking about Michelle. She's the only one here today taking new clients. MICHELLE! YOUR CLIENT . . . what's your name, baby?"

"Amena," I'd say to myself.

"What's your name?!"

"AMENA!"

"MICHELLE, YOUR CLIENT AMENA'S WAITING FOR

YOU!" they'd say while finishing their current client with hair-spray and oil sheen. "Sit right here at her station. She'll be right with you."

If you cannot speak before you're spoken to, if you cannot speak when spoken to, you will be Black Salon Embarrassed.

2. Be Careful Who You Speak For or Against

This is a tricky one and there's no way to know when you've hit one of these potential conversational pitfalls. In some salons, most of the stylists and clients are for Oprah/Michelle Obama/Barack Obama/Beyoncé/Cardi B/Nicki Minaj and, in the spirit of Benita Butrell from *In Living Color,* will not allow a word to be spoken against them. In every Black salon there will be some folks who are held as the Black Holy Grail. You just won't know *who* until you're in the middle of the conversation. To some folks, Will Smith can do no wrong, but some people will never forgive him for the slap. To some folks, Oprah is everything, but the hairstylist two stations down may not rock with Oprah because she wants to hear Oprah say Jesus instead of the Universe.

Don't voice any strong opinions until you hear who the stylists and clients near you are for. Save yourself a stressful appointment because you said you love Beyoncé and the hairstylist next to you just watched several hours of TikTok videos of Illuminati conspiracy theories.

3. Do Not Go to the Salon with Your Hair in a *Scattered* Situation

Some people were raised to wear clean drawers to go see the doctor. Not because the doctor is gon' see your drawers but because *you don't know* if the doctor will see your drawers and *what happens if they do?!*

Some people clean their houses before their house cleaner comes. This is similar to how it can feel going to a Black salon. I have been Black Salon Embarrassed about this many times. Mainly because I do what I'm gon' do to look cute until about two days before my next appointment. After that time, whatever happens to my hair is the responsibility of my hairstylist. If you make this choice, be prepared to at least get a strong up and down look and at most be clowned and talked about behind your back or in front of your face.

4. Have Strong Negotiation Skills

Almost every Black salon back in the day had some sort of hustler pass through. They sold bootleg copies of Black movies that were still in theaters. Sometimes they'd sell mixtapes, fish plates, and all sorts of things. If you don't have quick negotiation skills, say no to everything. You don't have time to inquire if the fish was farm raised or if the bootleg movie is in HD. You've got sixty seconds to not only decide if you want the hustler's wares, but also determine if you will stick with the price given to you and how quickly you will pay. And all of this is happening while your hairstylist talks to you about your split ends. It's just not the time for multitasking.

5. Do Not Make Drastic Hair Changes

If you have been getting a relaxer and have decided to go natural (or vice versa), if you've always worn your natural hair color and have decided to go blond, if you have long hair and have decided to cut it short, do not do this in an open salon with multiple stylists and clients unless you want unsolicited commentary about your hair or your life. Notice that when Bernadine went to Gloria in *Waiting to Exhale* to cut her long hair short, no one else was in the salon. This haircut was completed in the shadow of the day, like Nicodemus's visit to Jesus at night. If you are wanting to make a drastic hair change, talk to your stylist about this ahead of time or request an early appointment before the salon is full of folks, unless you want to hear:

- Why would you go and cut all that beautiful hair off?

- You wanna go natural? You like your hair like this?!

- You going back to the creamy crack?! *Black is beautiful!*

- Blond is for Mary J. Blige but it ain't for everybody!

- Baby, you okay? You going through a breakup? A divorce? You know how we change our hair when we going through things.

If you don't want to hear any of this, do not announce your drastic hair change to a full salon in the middle of the day.

6. Relax, Relate, and Release Your Attitude

Did you have a bad day? Your kids been getting on your nerves? Are you suffering from a relationship with a partner who ain't no good?! These are all understandable occurrences, but you will be better served not swinging your attitude around a Black hair salon like a reckless big set of hips. Do not walk into a Black hair salon thinking you are better than everyone there, or that the purpose of your hairstylist is to be "the help." You don't want to have too much attitude with someone serving you food, but you definitely don't want to have too much attitude with someone who can literally control whether you keep the hair you have or whether you walk out looking better than when you walked in. Be kind. Woosah. Be honest if it's been a rough day or if you're not up for conversation and ki-ki-ing during your appointment. A bad attitude can stink up the salon. Take a deep breath and focus your attention on today's episode of *The Young and the Restless* whether on TV or live in the salon.

7. If You Are a New Hairstylist or a Seasoned One, Know Your Limitations

Some hairstylists are good at color, some are good at cutting, some are good at trendy styles, some are good at old faithful styles. Know which category you fall in. If a client walks in and asks for a sew-in and you've never even sewn a button back on, if a client asks for a cut you've never done before, it's okay to let the client know they may be served better by another hairstylist. Honesty is better than you telling someone who has two inches of hair that you can give them a French roll for their high school reunion. Honesty is better than you giving someone a croissant or a cupcake when they asked for a French roll. Tell the truth and shame the devil. Or don't tell the truth and propel your client into the walk of shame from your chair into their real life. When other hairstylists walk by your chair while you're styling a client and are deathly silent or suck their teeth or ask, "Did you mean to do that?" take it as a cue. Stick to the rivers and lakes you're used to until you learn how to chase hair waterfalls.

These days whether I go to my regular hairstylist or my braider, I am going to a solo salon experience, with typically no more than three people present including me. No hustlers. No other stylists, booths, or stations. But the first thing I do when I walk in is speak. Black salons trained me right.

POETRY, CURLS, AND HOW TO DRESS WHEN YOU MEET TRACEE ELLIS ROSS

n 2019, I began the year at a Black woman retreat. We had sessions about business, about relationships, about finances. We also had breakout sessions and healing circles. I decided to attend the healing circle because I figured I could at least use a little healing. But I was cautious. My church upbringing taught me not to trust everybody's shondo or hee-bah-bah.

In the circle, any of us could share where we were wounded, where we felt we needed healing, and the leaders in the group could respond, as could other women in the circle. I raised my hand and shared how I was struggling working as an artist in such conservative and white spaces, how it was affecting my health and my personal life. I cried a lot of tears that needed a place to release.

The facilitator looked at me and said, "That space you're

working in? You need to get out. You cannot keep reentering spaces that traumatize you."

I knew I needed to get out of those spaces, but something about her words gave me permission to act. I left the retreat feeling encouraged, inspired, and rejuvenated, until I arrived home and felt the anxiety of actually doing what she said. I was in my late thirties. How could I start over? Where should I start? What should I do? My anxiety was so high I couldn't sleep. I felt stuck.

A couple of months later, I received an email through my website contact form. A creative agency was inquiring about the possibility of me writing a poetic voiceover for a Black celebrity client who was about to launch a natural hair care brand. *Celebrity?* I thought. These days *celebrity* is such a broad term, no longer a title that an external entity has to bestow upon you. It's now a term you can bestow upon yourself, which means I could be dealing with someone who decided one morning they were a celebrity. The whole thing smelled like a scam.

I forwarded the email to my now-manager, Celeste, and said, "Can you be my manager for twenty minutes and find out if this is legit?"

She wrote back and said, "This is definitely legit. They're asking for writing samples from you."

I submitted three poetry samples in written form plus videos of my performing them. I still wasn't sure what this whole thing was going to turn out to be about or if it was going to be real. I wasn't sure if they were going to want me to write a voice-over or if they might want me to be on camera too. Then we waited.

We didn't hear back for a couple of days and I thought maybe they went in a different direction, which is typically what creative agencies say when you don't get chosen for an opportunity. I thought maybe I was being considered alongside several other poets. I imagined my imaginary competition. I sized them up and I surmised they were better than me, more qualified, so I started eating cake to comfort my preemptive sorrow.

The next day Celeste messaged me back. "Hey, I'm emailing you a non-disclosure agreement. I need you to sign this NDA because the Black celebrity client wants to talk to you on the phone. But they can't talk to you on the phone and they can't tell us who the client is until you sign this NDA."

At the time, I was headed to a poetry performance in Winston-Salem, North Carolina, an hour or so from where my grandma and mom are from. My grandma is the star of our family, so anytime I had a gig close to her hometown, I simultaneously became a performing artist and a tour manager for my grandma. With my grandma and mom in tow, I was halfway to Winston-Salem when I received this message. I stopped off at a coffee shop and while my mom and grandma took a bathroom break, I read the NDA, which basically said I couldn't tell anybody what I was about to work on or who I would be working with. I downloaded the NDA, e-signed it, and sent it back.

A few minutes later, Celeste called me on the phone.

"Do you want to know who the Black celebrity client is?"

"I do," I said.

"Guess," she said.

"Oprah?"

"Nope."

"Beyoncé?"

"Nope."

"Michelle Obama?"

"Nope."

By this time my grandma and mom were back in the car.

"Okay, what rhymes with boss?"

"Diana Ross!" my mom said in the background.

"Your mom is close. It's Tracee Ellis Ross!"

I shut the car door and I ran around the front of the coffee shop. I'm pretty sure I yelled and joyfully cussed like my mom and my grandma couldn't hear me from inside the car.

The next day, I took the call in the car because my hotel room was now full of family who had come to visit my grandma. Tracee, her team, and the creative agency team joined the call. Tracee told me about PATTERN Beauty, a natural hair care brand she had been dreaming of and planning for over a decade. She wanted beautiful language to surround the brand as it launched into the world. She wanted to celebrate Black hair, Black culture, and Black legacy.

Right at the end of the call, Tracee said, "Amena, I should've started with this. Your work is truthful, soulful, full of joy, and full of lightness, and that is why I wanted to work with you on this project."

Cries. Faints. Wakes up. Cries some more.

We decided our next step was for Tracee, her team, and me to have more calls about what she wanted the poetic piece to say. And once the piece was written, she and I would meet in New York and review the piece together.

When I returned home to my office, I wrote "truthful, soulful, joyful, and light" on a Post-it. I still have that Post-it in my office to this day. Tracee had no idea how much my artist-self needed to hear her say those words. When Tracee said those words to me, I thought to myself, That's what I want my work to be doing. Here was this creative artist I looked up to, whose work I loved and respected, who was saying to me she could see my work doing the thing I had always hoped it would do.

I took all the words Tracee shared with me about her vision for PATTERN and I wrote a poem. Once the poem was finished, it was time for me to fly to New York to meet with Tracee and share the poem with her. She wanted us to review it together and collaborate in person. I was excited about the trip until it dawned on me, I was going to be meeting with Tracee Ellis Ross. In person.

How do you dress in front of fashion icon Tracee Thee Ellis Ross?! Do I have the clothes for this?! Do I have the budget for the clothes for this?! I didn't have money to buy anything new, so I went in my closet and over a period of days tried on every combination of clothes I had. I had to meet with her for two days, so I needed two solid outfits. I was certain I did not have the fashions or the fashion sense for this meeting. Dreadful. I wore what I had the best I could.

The first day I wore a black blouse tucked into high-waisted, black-on-black leopard print jeans and black boots. I stayed with a good friend, who could not believe I had the audacity to stay in her New York City apartment for free and still not tell her who the hell I was meeting. I told her I'd tell her as soon as I could, but I could not divulge the secret just yet. In my friend's guest room, I twisted my hair carefully the night before my first meeting with Tracee, hoping to reveal the perfect twist out in the morning. I had my eyebrows done. I couldn't figure out what to do with my nails. I couldn't afford to get them done so I manicured them neatly myself.

The morning of the meeting my twist out came out as close to perfection as I could get it. I applied my makeup, including a bold purple eyeshadow and magenta lipstick. I took the train to the creative agency's office, two hours early because I refused to be late. There was a coffee shop two doors down from the agency's building and I went in, not because I wanted or needed coffee but because I needed to hyperventilate for a few minutes.

One of the good things about New York City is the way people continue to go about their business. I sat down at a table and hyperventilated for a bit. A man walked up and asked was the other seat at my table free. I gestured for him to take a seat and continued to hyperventilate. He sat down and scrolled his phone, paying me no mind as a New Yorker is wont to do. After I felt I had done a good job hyperventilating it was time for me to head to the meeting.

I was still nervous that maybe this whole thing was a sham. All of my talks with Tracee and her team had been phone calls, not video calls. I'd heard her voice. I was sure it was her but as I walked into the building, I questioned myself. What if I was being catfished? What if I hadn't been talking to Tracee at all?! What if I was about to take an elevator ride to an abandoned floor of a New York building to discover a man with a hairy stomach and a scratchy voice sounding like the early scenes of a scary movie or a wild episode of *Fame*?

"Not the Tracy you were expecting, huh?" he'd say in a gruff voice.

But thankfully when the elevator opened up, I was not in an episode of *Fame* where the naïve dancer discovers she's been had. The creative agency was legit, and I could see Tracee meeting with her team in the boardroom. I was early enough that I had time to go to the bathroom and further freak out. I peed all I could pee. I checked my nostrils for boogers and stragglers. I patted my face with makeup. I touched up my lipstick. I went back to the lobby and someone from the agency came to get me to introduce me to Tracee.

Tracee greeted me with a hug and we both expressed how good it was to meet each other in person.

"I love your purple eyeshadow!" she said.

And in that moment, I might as well have won a fashion Oscar. A fashy. I don't know. I need to workshop this award name. I don't want it to be confused with an award for fascism instead of an award for fashion. We have enough of those going around. A Tracee. Maybe that's better. A Tracee is an award you receive when Tracee Ellis Ross says she likes anything about your fashion.

Steps to podium

"Wow! Tracee, thank you for presenting this award to me! Wow, I wasn't expecting this. As someone who only several years ago did not understand the difference between a winter shoe and an all-weather shoe, I'd like to dedicate this to all the not-so-fashion girlies. Who can't tell the difference between Balenciaga and Balmain. Who shop for budget and not for name brand. Who dress more for comfort than couture. This award is for us!

"I'd like to thank my mom for demonstrating the importance of a bold lip. I'd like to thank my sister for keeping me from buying the same ole shirt in a bunch of different colors. Thank you, Keda, for being willing to tell me when something I've tried on is ugly. I dress better because of you. I'd like to thank MAC Cosmetics for providing the purple eyeshadow for which I'm receiving this award. I'd like to thank the color purple, the shade and the book. I'd like to thank Alice Walker, Celie, and Shug Avery specifically. I'd like to thank Black Jesus from *Good Times* and Esther Rolle. Thank you!"

After I received my Tracee Award, Tracee and I sat down to review what I'd written. I read it aloud and then she read it aloud.

"This is fucking good!" she said.

Tracee Ellis Ross saying anything you've written is "fucking good" is also its own Tracee Award.

Steps to podium

"Wow, two awards in one day! Thank you to the academy and by that I mean Tracee. I'd like to thank Maya Angelou, Sonia Sanchez, Nikki Giovanni, Lauryn Hill, Missy Elliott, and

Black Thought for the inspiration to become a poet. I'd like to thank my mom for having such an amazing library that she inspired me to become a writer. I'd like to thank words and sentence structure. Special thank-you to jazz, hip hop, and couplets. Couldn't have done it without you!"

Tracee and I read through the piece again. She told me themes she'd love to see represented there. We talked about places we'd like to add and places we'd like to shorten. She asked me to update the draft and come back and meet with her again the next day.

I went back to my friend's place and wrote some more. For the second day, I wore a leopard cardigan I had picked up at Century 21, my then-favorite New York store, purple pants, and leopard flats. I pinned the top of my hair up and went with gold eyeshadow and gold lip gloss. I didn't hyperventilate this time. I went back to meet Tracee with the updated draft.

"This is it! This is beautiful. It's finished!" she said.

That piece became the PATTERN Beauty Manifesta, a piece that Tracee wanted to use as a part of the launch of the brand as well as a piece that would live as something that felt like it belonged to the PATTERN community, where people with curls, kinks, naps, and coils could feel seen, loved, and celebrated.

At the end of that meeting, I told Tracee how much I appreciated the opportunity, and she shared how much she appreciated working with me. As I was about to leave, my contact at the agency arrived to walk me out.

"How did y'all find me? What made you choose me?" I asked.

"Oh, we were looking on YouTube and there was a particular phrase related to natural hair that we were searching. Your video of 'Letter to My Hair' was the first thing to come up. It was supposed to be you."

My YouTube channel was not a bastion of views. It was

more of an archive of my work. It wasn't sensational but it represented my voice well. As a girl who grew up in a Pentecostal church, I felt a shout coming on, but I decided maybe in the lobby of this agency, in earshot of Tracee Ellis Ross, was not the place or the time. I shook her hand, thanked her, and took the elevator back down to the building lobby. Between walking out of the doors of the building into the busy Manhattan street and the turnstile of the train station, I began an ugly cry, a combination of Sofia from *The Color Purple* when she told Miss Celie she know'd there's a God, and Will Smith playing Chris Gardner in *The Pursuit of Happyness*, clapping his hands while crying and walking in just as busy of a New York City street as I was. I cried. I thanked God. And nobody in New York paid me no never mind.

I thought about how lost I'd felt a couple of months earlier, unsure of what was next for me, not being sure if there was a place for me. This moment, writing for what would become PATTERN Beauty, being awarded two Tracees, was such a great encouragement to me. There was a place for the work I was doing. There was a big world out there, a big sky for my wings, a big place for me to take flight. There were a lot of opportunities to come, and I didn't have to be stuck in a space that was not going to give me the freedom I wanted for myself.

Tracee performed the PATTERN Manifesta over a beautiful video directed by Micaiah Carter that celebrated Black hair and Black culture and introduced PATTERN Beauty to the world. Over the next few years, I collaborated with Tracee and the PATTERN team on many poetic pieces, as the PATTERN poetic partner, and these are still some of my favorite collaborations and creative work.

This moment proved to me direction can come from unexpected places. Also, if you are a freelancer, an entrepreneur, creative, or artist, stop reading this right now and go check and make sure when you fill out the form on your website, the emails actually come to you. Make sure your cute little contact form isn't going to spam when people email you, causing you to miss all sorts of opportunities.

Did you check the form on your website? Is it working? Okay whew, glad you're back.

I hope I have a moment in my career where I can give out some Amena Awards, for well-written poetry, or fresh sneakers, or a really delicious mac and cheese. As a two-time Tracee Award winner, I'm honored.

WASH DAY RITUAL

1. Light a candle.

2. Begin a meal that is low and slow.

3. Wash your hair, in the shower or in the sink like the women before you may have done.

4. Use a moisturizing shampoo, one that smells good to you. Rinse out the shampoo.

5. Apply a deep conditioner from the roots to the tips of your hair. Leave the conditioner on for way longer than the package says. Leaving conditioner on just a little too long is the equivalent of sprinkling Ajax in the tub as if the tub needs to "soak." We don't ask questions about why or how it works; we just know it does.

6.   Turn on a movie you've watched before. Or a movie you've never seen. Or a TV show you've been waiting to binge.

7.   Wash day can be a date with yourself if you let it.

8.   Rinse your conditioner out that you inevitably left on for hours because you fell asleep or went to run errands or got caught up on the phone talking to someone you like.

9.   Moisturize your hair and scalp. Like the women before you did. Don't rush. Take your time. Relish how your curls feel beneath your fingertips, the layers of textures. Explore your scalp like a treasure map.

10.   Apply your styling products. Maybe the ones you have in your cabinet you forgot about. Maybe the ones you just bought even though you know you have products in your cabinet that you forgot about.

11.   Twist, braid, coil, feel the oil on your fingertips.

12.   Wrap your hair in a luxurious silk or satin scarf.

13.   Remember your hair deserves love, care, and gentleness, and so do you.

PART 2

I HAVE BEEN MONOGAMOUS MY WHOLE LIFE BUT I'D CONSIDER POLYGAMY IF I COULD MARRY PROSCIUTTO

A COCKTAILS GIRL

am a late bloomer. I had my first drink at twenty-five years old. At twenty-one, instead of going out and having my first legal drink, I attended Bible study like a good church girl should. My first drink was a Riesling, when Riesling was having its day, the rosé of its time. Like when ordering Moscato was sophisticated. I was too green to appreciate a dry white wine or a full-bodied red wine, so Riesling seemed like the closest I could get.

My relationship to alcohol is one like the relationship you have with that distant cousin you saw sometimes growing up but never quite got to know. My mom enjoyed Coronas and margaritas in her pre-church era when she was still dancing in the clubs, but once my mom started going back to church, she quit social drinking altogether. The church I grew up in was contemporary but Pentecostal. Some things were decidedly sacred, and some things were hellishly sinful. Alcohol fell into the category of being highly flammable in the spiritual and physical sense. We were taught alcohol was all or nothing. A holy life dictated no alcohol, and a worldly life dictated too much alcohol. There was no in-between.

When I went to visit my dad, stepmother, and siblings for the summer, alcohol was casual, fun, and the life of the party. My dad and stepmother, both Air Force sergeants, liked to finish the day with a sip of Crown Royal or gin. They even had a bar in their home that they'd brought back from a duty station in Japan. I prayed that their souls might be saved.

Sometimes they hosted house parties for their friends, kickbacks where the drinks flowed, bid whist trash talking ensued, tables were slapped with dominoes, and after a while the children were sent to bed so the adults could enjoy a night free of worrying about what we might emulate or overhear.

When I left for college, many people thought I would move to Atlanta and immediately get turned out. Instead, as the rule follower I am, I went and found a campus ministry to be a part of and a church to join as soon as I could. Drinking wasn't allowed in our campus ministry or from the members in our church congregation because it could discourage people who weren't Christians from becoming Christian. It wasn't until I left the church that I decided I'd like to sip from the cup of lasciviousness myself before making my own decision about drinking.

Unfortunately, my first drink was a not so good occasion. I had been dating a guy. The marrying kind. We met at church, and he was one of the most eligible bachelors there. He was a few years older than me and ready to get married. I was in my twenties and just discovering I was cute. I had been hired for my first real job out of college, and he wanted to take me to dinner to celebrate. He took me to a nice restaurant that doubled as a jazz club. He knew this was my first drink and wanted to also celebrate this with me.

I took a gulp of my Riesling and a bite of my salmon and promptly told him I only saw us being friends. I know Jamie Foxx and T. Pain have extolled the reasons why one could blame it on the Grey Goose or on the Patrón, but could I blame it on the Riesling? Could Riesling affect my reasoning? I am generally a person who has a hard time lying, but a few sips of alcohol really turn me into a truth teller.

I finished my glass of Riesling and my salmon cooked to medium because I'm a sophisticated lady, told him I hope we stay in touch as friends and friends only, and all of this before the check arrived. He was kind, so he paid the check since he'd invited me on the date and promised it would be his treat, but his eyes told me his heart was broken. The food and drink were delicious, but my choice to end things with this man in this way after we sat for such a nice meal . . . was . . . in bad taste? Thank you for appreciating my pun intended.

For my next birthday, I organized what felt like my first grown and sexy birthday, a gathering of my friends at a tapas bar. Nothing said grown and sophisticated like eating small plates of expensive food for your birthday. I was dating a guy who I'd had a crush on for a while. He was attractive but also chronically late for dates and a terrible gift giver. For my birthday that year I'd bought myself my first Mac laptop. When he came to pick me up for my party, he handed me his birthday gift and wanted me to open it.

"I got you something to go with your new laptop," he said, beaming with pride.

I couldn't imagine what that could be. A laptop sleeve? A laptop case? A laptop bag? The little gift bag he'd handed me was way too small for that. When I removed the tissue paper, I discovered a thumb drive. 156 MB.

"You could use it for your files and stuff," he said and smiled.

What files? Two Word docs and six pictures? What could I even fit on this thumb drive?! But I smiled and said thank you because my mom raised me to have manners. When we arrived at the party I gathered with my friends in the reserved lounge for private parties, which had cool couches, armchairs, and ottomans, much better furniture than I had in my apartment at the time. My date told me he invited one of his best friends, a best friend whose name I'd heard but who I'd never met in person.

When my date's friend walked in, I wasn't expecting him to be fine as all outdoors! My date was good-looking but somehow his friend was even better-looking! His friend walked in, told me happy birthday, and handed me a long gift bag, so long I couldn't imagine what could have been in it. When I removed the tissue, I discovered he'd gifted me a bottle of Yellow Tail wine. I didn't know anything about wine. All I knew was this fine ass man thought I was the type of classy lady who should receive wine for her birthday, and based on that Yellow Tail had to be an expensive, exclusive vintage wine. I beamed with pride and said thank you and thought to myself if I had met them at the same time I would have definitely chosen the friend.

My friends sang "Happy Birthday" to me as I blew out the candle of my classy lady dessert. As my date was driving me home from what had turned out to be a wonderful birthday party, I could not stop talking about the wine his friend had given me. I'd just moved into my first apartment and now I would be a classy lady who would have wine on hand for guests. I must have gone on for a while because I noticed my date had grown quiet. So I stopped talking and we both listened to the sound of his tires on the highway. After a long period of silence, he said, "So you ain't like that thumb drive I gave you?" He missed so many social cues.

In the years after that I stuck with wine, moving on to try Cabernet, Malbec, and Chardonnay. In some ways, imagining myself a *Real Housewives* cast member who always had the perfect wine to serve over gossip with her friends on a yacht or a high-rise condo or the glorious back deck of a vacation home. I eventually understood wine wasn't just good because it was sweet. I eventually understood that certain wines paired well with certain foods. I eventually understood that Yellow Tail is not a classy or sophisticated wine, it's a cheap to affordable wine you can get at the grocery store, but even this in retrospect did not change how fine my date's best friend was.

After a few years I started dabbling in cocktails. Instead of scared straight I was drinking scared. I didn't like the feeling of losing my inhibitions. Wine seemed to only dull them, not cause me to dance on top of tables in a bar like I was starring in *Coyote Ugly*. But then I became a foodie and came to understand the amount of culinary creativity that goes into a cocktail. That cocktails go beyond margaritas and daiquiris. I gained some friends who were cocktail connoisseurs and they took me along for the ride. I learned about pestle and mortar, the importance of crushed herbs, orange peels, liquor-infused cherries, international liquor, local liquor. I started ordering a cocktail instead of a glass of wine. I started staying awake for social activities. I started imagining myself the kind of Real Housewife that has a signature drink (three lemons carcass out?! Hello, Dorit?!).

My career started expanding into the kind of white church people who don't just drink wine during communion. I started getting invited to things they called "after-parties" but were really cocktails and guitar playing. It is then I realized I didn't know how to pace myself. Back then I'd order a cocktail and down it with the same speed a teenager would drink Dr Pepper with free refills.

At this event, I had done an hour-long poetry set. I'd talked about spirituality, friendships, and romantic relationships. I almost brought up a questionable topic while onstage, but I held back remembering these are church folks and thinking maybe I should save this type of conversation for the group chat. But after a too quickly downed cocktail at the "after-party" my true thoughts were revealed.

One of the women at the after-party asked, "When you were onstage, you looked like you were about to say something, but you didn't. What were you going to say?"

Normal me, usual me, me with only a few waters under her belt would have skirted away from this topic, would have pulled her to the side in a quiet corner where I could whisper my thoughts. But tipsy me, after one strong cocktail, had no such restraint.

"Balls. I was going to talk about balls," I said.

Her eyes went big.

"I mean, here I am raised in church and people are giving me all this advice about fixing my husband's plate and wearing sexy lingerie, but nobody thought about telling me about balls?!"

She shuffled her straw in her drink.

"What a weird thing to encounter for the first time with no warning?! Can you imagine if you'd never felt the texture of a basketball in your life and someone just tossed it to you one night and said, 'Here, this is yours now!'?!" I said.

At this point I realized it wasn't just one woman I was talking to. I was talking to a table full of women, most of them pastors' wives.

"She's really gonna keep talking about this, huh?" one of them whispered to the other. But my bionic cocktail-powered ears heard her clearly.

And this is where tipsy Amena started getting frustrated.

"I mean, you've all got husbands. I don't know why you're so uncomfortable. You see balls every day! Don't you think they're strange?! Don't you think it's weird how men call women temperamental, but they can't even know what exactly their balls are doing at any given moment of the day?! Their balls are temperamental!"

This last paragraph is a loose translation of what I can remember saying, what I was thinking, and what my sister-in-law could remember me saying when she overheard me a table away. She walked over and poked me in the shoulder with her finger and said, "Let's go. We're going back to the hotel."

And that's how I learned that drinking cocktails causes me to talk incessantly about balls. I have presented a thesis on balls after a drink. I have touted a technique for how to handle balls when you encounter them after having a drink. I have subsequently told others while sober that I couldn't have a drink because I might incessantly talk about balls.

Even after all these years I still can't handle my liquor well. My husband and I went on a date once, and I ordered a cocktail from the menu that sounded amazing. The waitress alerted me that my cocktail came with a sidecar. I had no idea what to expect. When would my church girl ass have learned about a sidecar? I'd barely learned not to drink all the wine at a wine tasting. The only mental reference I could conjure for a sidecar was from *Hawaii Five-0*, the original one. I said sure because I didn't want to appear in another episode of Black Girl Who's Never Been Places.

She brought me a full-sized cocktail and a mini carafe, the sidecar, to refill it. I was having a good time with good food and flirting with my husband, so I drank my drink and its sidecar. By the time we paid for the bill, something was wrong. My eyeballs felt like they had gone for a swim and didn't invite the rest of my body. I imagined myself as stiff as a diving board, hoping my husband would pick me up and carry me to the car the same way he'd carry a piece of lumber.

"I need to go home," I said.

"You okay?" he said.

"Yeah, but I need to go somewhere I can lie down in a straight line."

Despite what Jamie Foxx and T. Pain sang through auto-tune, I try not to blame it on the alcohol. Not the breakup. Not the incessant conversation about balls. Not thinking a grocery store wine was the same as a vintage wine from an obscure winery in the south of France. I drink sparingly and occasionally. I've learned the importance of alternating water in between my cocktails. I've learned I will not drink anything neat or on the rocks. It's an elderberry rosemary lemonade orange bitters cacao essence rum smoke for me.

I've learned what I love most about a good cocktail is the artistry, the layers of flavoring, the herbs, bitters, spirits, fruits that can take my tastebuds on a journey. I've also learned to sip a cocktail, to take my time. There's no need to rush. There's plenty of time to talk about balls. Oh, and I never drink the sidecar. I'm riding shotgun or passenger seat when it comes to a drink, no more sidecars for me.

BECOMING A GOOD COOK

wasn't always a good cook. It didn't come easily or naturally to me. Being a good cook in my family is a status I worked hard to earn.

I remember peeking over the stove and watching what my grandmother and great-grandmother were cooking. They were both good cooks. In a Black house in the South, where they were from, you might say they could *burn*, they put their *foot* in them greens, in that barbecue, in that cake. My earliest kitchen memories were standing at their side, barely tall enough to see the stovetop.

These were North Carolina women. Frying chicken, making chicken pastry, baking cakes, frying fish, stewing collard greens and cabbage and butter beans. I was too young to think to ask for recipes. I was also too young to understand they probably didn't have one for most things.

My earliest memory of being in the kitchen with my mom was baking chocolate chip cookies on Friday nights just in time to watch *Miami Vice* on television, which for my mom was just in time to watch Detective Ricardo Tubbs, who was played by Philip Michael Thomas. When a Black man has three names, he is always fine as hell. André Three Thousand. Michael B. Jordan. James Earl Jones (check the pictures of Young James. I said what I said!). John David Washington and his daddy Den Zel Washington. This is just the truth, I don't make up the rules. The last batch of our cookies always burned because my mom got caught up watching Philip Michael Thomas and the show.

I returned to my mom's baking tradition by learning how to bake banana bread and cupcakes in high school. My high school in San Antonio, Texas, was a big sports school, so I started baking cupcakes in our school colors for pep rally Fridays.

When I visited my dad, stepmother, and siblings during the summers growing up, my dad taught me how to make cream of mushroom pork chops, how to fry chicken and pork rinds. My stepmother taught me how to make biscuits and Tennessee sausage and gravy, and she taught me how to make her famous cornbread dressing.

In college, I only lived in an apartment for one year and I can hardly tell you what the kitchen in that place even looked like. The rest of my college years were spent in a dorm with a meal plan, so I barely cooked anything for myself outside of microwave popcorn. It wasn't until I was in my mid-twenties working my first real job that I started to wonder if I should learn how to cook.

When I moved into my first apartment, I owned a hand-me-down bed frame and mattress, a secondhand, curvy, uncomfortable couch, a bubble TV, and a few IKEA plates. I had been living with housemates prior to this, so I could depend on their shared furniture and kitchen appliances, but now in my first apartment and in my first corporate job I needed to fill the rest of my home myself.

I'd been working in corporate America for over a year, and I was sure I wanted out. My apartment complex offered me a discount on a one-bedroom, one-bathroom apartment if I was willing to move into one that did not have the connections for a washer and dryer. This might seem like a precarious choice; indeed, it was, but I thought to myself, in a year or so, I'm going to quit this corporate job I hate and become a full-time artist. I needed to cut myself any kind of break I could in advance. I figured I had enough friends and family in the area to borrow the use of a washer and dryer, and I could always resort to the apartment laundry or a laundromat if I was prepared to stand guard over my clothes and detergent and fight for my life and their cleanliness.

I don't know if it was the quaintness of my little faux granite countertops in my apartment, but I started feeling the need to get real domesticated. I'd always wanted to get married, but growing up in a Black evangelical, Pentecostal, charismatic church, plus growing up in the era of the book *I Kissed Dating Goodbye,* made the path to dating and marriage fraught with missteps. We were told not to date too young, not to be unequally yoked, not to kiss, not to have sex, which basically meant if you wanted to be in a relationship you'd have to hope that one of your friends would somehow convert over into a fiancé right quick.

I assessed myself. I felt like I looked pretty good. I dressed all right. I was a great conversationalist. I had morals, ethics, and religion. There were two things I didn't have: a sex life and strong cooking abilities. I was too afraid to get a sex life, so I figured the best way to jump-start a path to marriage was learning how to cook.

Over the years, I'd picked up a few things. I learned how to cook spaghetti, lasagna, spaghetti, tuna fish salad (does this even count as "cooking"?!), meatloaf, and spaghetti. But I didn't know how to cook any of the soul food staples. So I went to the expert, my Grandma Bert, short for Bertha Mae. To our family she is Grandma Bert, Aunt Bert, Cousin Bert. To church folks, she is Mother Lee. I went to her with a request.

"Grandma, if the way to a man's heart is through his stomach, I'm never gon' get there like this," I said. "Can you teach me how to make some of the soul food dishes?"

Her eyes lit up as if she had been waiting for me to ask this for years, as if she could now open the book of magic and spells and show me potions, recipes, and divinations.

We started with collard greens. There was no recipe for this. I had to get in the kitchen next to her, watch her cook, and take notes as best I could. We started with bunches of collard greens, leaves still on the stem.

"Now, Mena, first thing you wanna do is soak these collards in salt water," she said.

She stopped up the right side of the sink, sprinkled Morton's salt under running water as we took each leaf and submerged it.

"Now the reason why you wanna do a saltwater soak is to make sure you take care of any bugs that might still be on the greens," she said.

Bugs?! I thought but didn't say anything.

After the collards were thoroughly soaked, we rinsed them again in the left side of the sink. She tore the leaves from the stems with her hands and showed me how to do the same. We rolled up the leaves into thin rolls and then sliced the rolls into one-inch segments, slicing them just so, to provide a proper mouthfeel, even though my grandma didn't know what mouthfeel meant.

Once that was done, she took me through the seasoning process. The smoked turkey necks (that she made sure to remind me used to be smoked ham hocks before she started trying to eat healthier), the salt, the pepper, the garlic, the little bit of sugar. The result was delicious, just as I remembered her collard greens to be.

A couple of weeks later we met up again for a collard green cook down, this time with bags of collard greens. Grandma poured the bag into the right side of the sink that was already filling with salted water. When it was time to rinse, Grandma picked out all the stalks.

"I don't like stalks in my greens," she said, eyeing me strongly to let me know how important this was.

After rinsing, we seasoned the greens, stewing them, cooking them down until they were a combination of tenderness and the perfect bite. From there my next charge was to cook them on my own and bring them back to her to taste.

The soaking went a little differently in my small first apartment kitchen. I didn't have two sides of a sink and instead had one basin. I soaked, salted, picked out the stalks, seasoned, stewed, until I got as close to what I could remember of what she'd taught me.

I put a small amount in a plastic bowl and took it over to her home for her to taste.

"Now, you got the texture right, but it tastes a little too salty," she said.

For weeks I took her notes and tips and went back into my kitchen to keep trying the collard greens, until finally, she ate what I made with no commentary but some mm-hmms and an empty dish. When she handed the tasting dish back to me clean with no notes, I knew I'd made it.

We moved on to mac and cheese. We discussed which five cheeses were necessary, sharp cheddar cheese being the most important, but also needing mild cheddar, Colby, Monterey Jack, and cream cheese. Plus, the use of Velveeta to bind the dish together.

This is really one of the holy grails of soul food cooking. The phrase "I don't play about this one" applies to the people you love and applies to mac and cheese. There are rules to this. The mac and cheese maker in the family must be apprenticed. You must know from whence they received their mac and cheese recipe. Was it bestowed upon them? Did they learn at the knee or hip of an elder in the family? Had their mac and cheese been tested and tasted? By how many people? And by whom? Had it been tested by someone whose palate we trusted?

I followed my grandma's recipe in the kitchen with her, some parts written down and some parts only known to her memory. We boiled the macaroni noodles, and after draining away the hot water once they were done, poured them into the largest mixing bowl we could find. My grandma put butter and cream cheese in with the noodles and stirred until the hot noodles melted the butter and cream cheese. Next, she cheesed the macaroni to her heart's content, mixing the various cheeses and a can of Campbell's cheese soup in place of the Velveeta, seasoning with salt and pepper to taste. The last step was to pour a bit of milk into this mixture. No measuring cup. No tablespoons. Just alternating pouring and stirring until the mac and cheese was moisturized but not too soupy. Tasting and cheesing in between. When the mac and cheese tasted just right, we poured all the contents in our mixing bowl into a casserole-sized pan and topped the mac and cheese with more shredded cheese, placing the mac and cheese in the oven to bake until the cheese sauce was bubbling in between the noodles, until the cheese on top was just beginning to caramelize. The final result was delicious, so good that I questioned my ability to reproduce these results in my own kitchen.

I tried anyway, various versions over a period of weeks. Took the dish back to my grandmother and heard "too dry," "too soupy," "not enough seasoning," until finally after a few tries she returned my tasting dish back to me clean and gave me a nod of approval.

We followed this process with cabbage and rutabagas and rice and gravy and any other family or Southern sides we could think of. I imagined myself cooking a big spread for some fine ass man I had a crush on, how I'd woo him with my tender, seasoned collard greens, delectable mac and cheese, and immense knowledge of all the lyrics of "Gangsta's Paradise."

That first year in my first apartment was glorious. I bought bookshelves, kitchen appliances, and a dinette table that my grandma agreed to pay for half of. I learned to cook. I went to concerts. I went on dates. But the day finally arrived where I said enough is enough to my boring day job and I quit. I thought I was just quitting my day job so I could work for myself and build my artist career. What I didn't realize is I was also quitting going to concerts and going out to eat with my friends. *Because I could not afford the tapas restaurant anymore.*

Being broke is the gap between the money you make and the bills and expenses you have to pay.

I experienced being broke growing up, this is how I learned to make tuna salad, egg salad, chicken salad, and bologna sandwiches. But being broke in my adulthood hit me differently because it was now up to me to feed myself.

I started with inviting my friends over when they wanted to go out. It turned out Yellow Tail wine and a boring dish of spaghetti was not that exciting to my friends. In the rare times I did go out to eat, all I could think was, *Could I make this at home?*

I've loved Sonic since I was in high school, when it was right across the street from campus. It's where we went after school, before a football game, after a football game. I went there on my first date and my drink of choice was a strawberry limeade. My first date ordered a cookies-and-cream milkshake. We tasted each other's drinks, and to my church girl mind we might as well have kissed. Sonic is for celebrations, for straight A's, for getting a raise, for finally being able to afford cable. But alas I went so broke after quitting my job, I could not afford Sonic. Not even a limeade.

And you might be saying, limeades are not that expensive. Yeah, but when you're broke and you're having to choose between keeping the lights on or going out to eat, then you will learn quickly that maybe a can of Shasta and one container of frozen strawberries and one lime can get you further than buying a Sonic strawberry limeade every time you want one.

The other restaurant I loved at the time was Maggiano's. It was as if Olive Garden had decided to grow up and wear a fedora now. Sometimes my mom would treat me to Maggiano's because she could probably tell by the shifty look in my eyes and my refusal to replace my threadbare coat that I was not in the best of times. I looked at the menu and my favorite dish, chicken marsala, cost almost $20. The next time I got paid from one of the low-paying side hustles I'd picked up, I looked up a chicken marsala recipe on Andre 3000's internet, went to the store, and purchased thinly sliced chicken breast, mushrooms, Marsala wine, and pasta and went to town building my own cheaper version of Maggiano's. *And life hack:* I didn't have just one portion of chicken marsala, I could eat it for *days* for a little less than I paid for one serving in the restaurant.

The Cooking School of Being Broke taught me some lessons. I didn't learn how to make a beef Wellington, but I learned how to make a dollar stretch upward dog, downward dog, all the warriors, and any other way that could carry me and that dollar to my next paycheck. I learned how to make a mean chicken marsala and a really good lasagna. I learned how to cook black-eyed peas to go with my collard greens on New Year's.

During my broke years, I met Matt, a tall white man with red hair and freckles, who I had no idea would become my husband. We started dating in the summer and by the time the fall arrived not only were things getting serious, but I was also finally making a bit more money. Our first Thanksgiving as a couple, Matt's parents went out of town for the holiday. His younger brother was staying in town for work, and since we were talking every day on the phone for hours, he told me, "I decided to stay in town for the holiday since my brother will be here." As soon as he said this, visions of dancing candied yams and boogie-ing bundles of mac and cheese started tootsie rolling in my head. I put my hands on my hips, hit a superhero stance, and decided I should host and cook for Thanksgiving. Hadn't I been trained and apprenticed for this moment?!

I didn't make Matt any promises. I called my mom first since she usually hosted Thanksgiving at her home. When I described the situation to her, and asked if I could host Thanksgiving for her, my sister, and my grandma, as well as Matt and his brother, at my current place, she said of course. At the time I was living in the house of a friend of mine, and she was gone for the holidays. She had a large dining room table and a big kitchen, so I asked her if she would be okay with me hosting a small holiday gathering while she was gone, and she agreed.

Then I called my grandma. I had a place secured. My mom approved of adding additional guests. Now, I needed to talk food. What dishes did we need for Thanksgiving? Greens? Mac and cheese? I could make those. My grandma approved. Candied yams? Yes, my grandma said, definitely. My mom volunteered to make the turkey, and I decided to add my stepmother's cornbread dressing to the menu. I called Matt back and told him the plan, and he and his brother were happy to come over and have as much of this food as they could.

Previous years, my attempting the Thanksgiving sides had been purely experimental; now I was agreeing to be *the one* to make the sides *and* I had invited guests. I'd arrived at the foyer of the Black Southern Woman Hall of Fame; the crown of you-can-now-cook-for-the-family had been bestowed upon me.

I went grocery shopping. I cooked and cleaned for days. I candied the yams, stewed the greens, and mac'd the cheese. Thanksgiving Day, we set the table, and I stood there beaming in front of my family, my new boyfriend, and my new boy-friend's brother. I received rave reviews, which came in the form of moans, grunts, forks clinking on plates, and clean plates in the dishwasher. I felt like I had somehow graduated. That even though I had been a full-fledged adult for years, with one nod from my grandma and a smile from my mom I had become officially grown!

I relished my early old Black auntie status. I sat on the couch and watched TV after everyone had eaten seconds and the kitchen had been cleaned. I felt triumphant and tired. All of a sudden, I felt really tired. Exhausted. I didn't let on, as every-one fixed their to-go plates, and as I walked them out the door, I was starting to feel a little out of it. I tried to reason my way through this. *It's probably logical for me to feel out of it. I just hosted my first Thanksgiving. I spent the last two days cooking. I'm probably just tired*, I thought. So, I went to bed hoping to feel better in the morning.

I woke up the next morning and my throat felt like its own version of *Knives Out*. I felt like there were daggers, needles, and ice picks scratching my throat away. My throat felt like it was on fire in the worst way. Being the daughter of a nurse, I assumed this must be strep, but I couldn't be sure.

So I called Matt and told him my throat hurt so bad, and I wasn't sure what was wrong. He said, "I'm coming to get you!" and in between my pain-ridden throat and when he arrived to pick me up, I thought, *I'm going to marry this man!* He picked me up. I called my mom and told her we were headed to urgent care. When I arrived at urgent care, the nurse said, "Yep, you have mono." Somehow, I managed to skip getting mono as a teenager, but at thirty years old, I had decided to get mono for the first time after hosting and cooking my first Thanksgiving.

This was taking away some of my cool in my relationship to my new boyfriend. Now, thankfully, Matt and I were friends for two years before we started dating each other. I'd been hanging out with him when I was wearing sweatpants and a raggedy T-shirt. But there I was in the car with my new boyfriend in the parking lot of Walmart, where I was picking up the meds I had to take for mono. It took me weeks to feel like my normal self.

When my throat was no longer sore. When I could breathe normally. I basked in my newfound status. I had cooked all the Thanksgiving sides and had not only received the approval of my mom, grandma, and sister, but also received the approval of my man and his brother. Ever since that Thanksgiving, I have been called upon by my family and extended family to whip up some candied yams, bring some mac and cheese, bake a sweet potato pie. Our house is now the place where we host Thanksgiving and Christmas. Where we fry fish on Juneteenth. Where I taught my sister how to cook the soul food staples for her boo.

I have learned to cook the way of my ancestors, with the best quality ingredients I can find, sometimes making do with what I have in my refrigerator or in my cabinets, or on what a limited budget will allow me, as the Cooking School for Being Broke taught me, learning to adapt my recipes and my life. Learning when to ask for help and when to kick everybody out of the kitchen. Learning when to rest and put my feet up. Learning how to not wear myself out cooking to the point that I'd get mono. Again.

The kitchen has always been a healing place for me. When I return to my kitchen, I return to myself, following a recipe that is my mother's, my father's, my stepmother's, my grandmother's, or my great-grandmother's. Learning to make recipes of my own. I find joy and curiosity in my kitchen, a willingness to follow a recipe and the opportunity to rebel against it. I cook food. I fix plates. I make delicious mistakes and sometimes mistakes that are not so delicious. In my kitchen now, I gather myself. I gather my family and my friends. I gather with those who have gone on before me. And the results are healing, hilarious, and delicious.

OUR OWN POTLUCK

Black women
Let's gather our love for each other
And find a meeting place
The table
The kitchen
The porch
The worn couch in the living room
The flesh underneath our arms
The curls at the nape of our necks

Let us bring our souls and hips to our own potluck
I will bring my ability to find humor in just about
    anything
And you
You will bring your shyness, your softness

And you
You will bring your takes-no-bullshit attitude
And you
You will bring your singing voice that pierces through the
    air like the first morning light of the sun
And you
You will bring greetings and say a prayer
Of blessing
Of lament
Of love
Of grace

We will spend time saying their names
The Black women and Black trans women who were taken
    from us
We will hold their names close to our collarbones
We will let their names rest in the silence of our breath
And we will fight for them

We will then speak our own names to each other
To the flowers as they remind us we still bloom
To our bellies as they remind us our bodies are worthy

We will bump hips trying to set the table
We will gather ourselves to heal
To remember

We will touch shoulders
And find ourselves in each other's smiles
Pass me a plate, sis
Pass the peace

FOODS I HAVE
FALLEN IN LOVE WITH

have been in love several times in life and most of those times were with food. *I love food.* I love to cook, but I love eating the best. Food is pleasure and pleasure is me. I have also had several minor car accidents and one of them was due to a delicious, life-changing, in-season pear that distracted me from driving and caused me to puncture my tire on a curb. This is the reason I no longer eat and drive.

Here is a list of a few of my favorite food loves. Full stomach. Clear plate. I choose. Or whatever you say when you watch my version of *Friday Night Lights,* which would be obviously called *Friday Night Bites.*

Fried Chicken

Growing up, I had two very distinct fried chicken experiences: the fried chicken cooked at home and the fried chicken we picked up on the way home from something else. The fried chicken cooked at home with my family was typically fried by my grandma. She fried chicken so good I asked her to fry chicken for me and my friends when I turned sixteen *and my friends still talk about that chicken*, like it was a spiritual, mythological experience.

But when my grandma wasn't frying chicken, she was picking it up from a fast-food place. When I was growing up there were only three places to do this: Church's, Kentucky Fried Chicken, and Popeyes. A Black family's loyalty to one of these places depended on a few things: region and level of desired spice. These are two things you can also list about yourself in a dating app.

My family is from North Carolina, so we weren't big spice people. We kept the requisite hot sauce around, but this was mostly for other Black people that might come to visit and subsequently shame you for your lack of hot sauce or for your choice of hot sauce.

We were a KFC family. I now question our trust in this older, jovial white man's ability to fry the chicken, but I believe the eleven herbs and spices were very convincing. Surely if he understood the need for this many herbs and spices, his original recipe could be trusted?

The convenience of being able to pull up to a drive-through and order a bucket of chicken with mashed potatoes and coleslaw as sides on a Sunday afternoon, where we had already spent enough time in church as if we were clocking in at our full-time job, was worth it in my grandmother's eyes and the eyes of her children and grandchildren.

One of the bonds my husband and I share in our interracial relationship is our Southern upbringing. We both moved around a lot but spent most of our time in the South, eating Southern food. My husband's favorite food is fried chicken. He and my grandmother take turns seeing who cleaned the bones of the chicken the best after a meal.

When we first got married, I wasn't pressed to learn to fry chicken. My grandmother could fry chicken and my mother-in-law could fry chicken. But after a few years I decided since this is my husband's favorite food maybe I should learn how to cook it.

I gathered tips from all the fryers on both sides of the family: my dad, my grandmother, my mother-in-law, my husband's aunt. I started with wings. And I will not participate in an argument here about drums and flats. But it will always be drums for me, thank you. I learned how to fry wings and then I moved up to drumsticks. When I mastered that, I moved up to thighs and breasts. Hello. This is still a conversation about chicken. Let's get back on track.

Frying chicken felt like an important task I needed to know how to do well. In the Black Southern woman's handbook, you must be prepared for last-minute visitors that may need a quick meal, a hungry preacher who may wind up with their legs underneath your dining room table after church, a cadre of civil rights activists who need to strategize how to combat racism while you heat up the frying oil. Frying chicken is a useful life skill!

Some of the best marriage advice I received was that there is more than one way to hang curtains and truly there are many right ways to fry chicken. Sometimes I fry with an egg dredge and then flour. These days I fry with a hot sauce marinade and then flour. My Dutch oven becomes its own version of a Fry Daddy. I let the windows up and go to work.

If fried chicken is done right, it will taste good steaming hot or chilled and cold. The perfection of a crispy, breaded fried outside and tender moist chicken on the inside is a *food of the gods.* I said what I said!

Hoagies

It's really hard to mention this without thinking of my first exposure to the power of a hoagie on a Black family television show, centered around a comedian whose predatory behavior has really complicated my memories. But yes, this was my first time hearing about hoagies. It would be many years into my adulthood before I was able to try one myself.

I took my first trip to Philadelphia for work to emcee an event. After three days of nonstop talking, greeting, and high-fiving, I decided to reward myself with some local Philly cuisine. I Yelped and found a local butcher/convenience store that also under the cover of night and day sold amazing hoagies. I ordered mine and a bag of Utz potato chips, grabbed my hoagie to go, and took it back to the hotel.

Some friends of mine were also at the conference, and my phone was ablaze with texts inviting me to dinner, inviting me to after-parties, inviting me to events, kickbacks, get-togethers. I undressed from my event clothes and took my bra off—which was the true sign I was in for the night, because in what world would I put my tiddies back in an uncomfortable sling. I put on my pj's and thought of one of Philly's most famous singers, Jill Scott. In her song "The Way," she wakes up, smiles, straightens up, gets dressed, makes herself breakfast (*griiiiiiiits*), goes to work, thinking about the way this man loves her. By the time we get to the second verse, she is leaving work inundated with invitations from her girls to go out. I texted my friends the equivalent of Jill's "Naw girl! Really! Get your groove on," except it was a sandwich instead of a man that would be taking up my time.

I love to eat in bed, but I especially love to eat in bed in a hotel. There is a trick to eating well in bed. First, you must endeavor to not get crumbs in between the sheets, shoutout to the Isley Brothers. This requires you either eat on top of the comforter or duvet. Or, and this method is my favorite, you get in bed, roll the covers up to your neck, place a hotel towel landscape from your neck to your waist, take your hoagie out of the plastic bag, place your plastic bag on top of the towel, unwrap your hoagie, and place half of it on your chest.

Many television shows and movies have displayed the moment a mother births a child and the child is laid on her chest. This is a primal and momentous occasion. Second to that or equal to that, depending on who's doing the ranking, is the feeling of clutching a delicious hoagie to your chest as you prepare to devour it in the hotel bed of your choice. No crying. No labor pains. Just mayo and joy.

I opened the hoagie that had already been cut in half and nearly drooled at the tender squeeze of mayo that ended up on my fingers. I dove into that sandwich, placed between two perfect pieces of Italian bread, drizzled with a heavenly manifestation of herbs, vinegar, and oil, teeming with nearly every Italian meat known to humanity. That day my life was changed. That day I became a girl who loved sandwiches. I dreamed of someday having a secret food blog called *Sandwich Bitch*, where all I did was travel around the country and eat good ass sandwiches in bed, in the car, or wherever my life was taking me. I could eat sandwiches in private and in public. I could eat sandwiches with other people. I could become a sandwich swinger, where we each ordered different sandwiches but tasted each other's.

And this leads me to my next love . . .

Prosciutto

I met prosciutto in a sandwich. Delicious, tender, and salty. Ours was a love at first bite. But we met in a busy sandwich where prosciutto had to share my attention with delicious bread and other meats and cheese. Our relationship bloomed when I had isolated time to enjoy prosciutto on a charcuterie board, where it deserved all my attention. I could pair it with a fancy cheese. I could pair it with dried apricots or a lovely jam. These days if I spy a menu and I see prosciutto as an ingredient in a dish, I'm going for it! I'm making it happen! Prosciutto has always been good to me! Lavish even. Luxurious!

Chicago Hot Dog

I got the worst case of food poisoning in my life after eating a Chicago hot dog and here's the thing. It was the best hot dog I'd ever had in my life! I had been on tour with a band, and my husband and I had only been married for a few months at the time. We met up in Chicago after two weeks away from each other and decided to not only have our first big married fight but also catch a vicious case of food poisoning.

You do not want to spend your last night with your person, after you haven't seen them in weeks, saying things like, "Well no, no, you misunderstood me, what I was trying to say . . ." and then running off to the bathroom to question if your organs will indeed stay inside your body.

For many years after this, I swore off hot dogs. At a cook-out, at a kid's birthday party, I just couldn't handle it. Years later my husband and I took a trip to Chicago with better communication skills and food recommendations from Chicago friends. I went to Portillo's to try and see if hot dogs and I could be friends again and *my god tuh-day*, Chicago hot dogs are life-changing when you don't have food poisoning and when you are not arguing with your spouse.

The celery salt, the sport peppers, the tomatoes, the pickle, the poppy seed bun. My my my! I can see why Johnny Gill said that! If a Chicago hot dog put on a red dress, slipped on high heels, and wore a sweet vinegar perfume, I'd give that Chicago hot dog the best night of its life!

On the Merits of Takeout

I like to eat food while I'm wearing slouchy pajamas and no bra. If I could have all food brought to me to eat in my home, in my comfy clothes without having to put my tiddies up in a sling, I would do it. I long to live a life of community service, but also room service.

This started on my birthdays in my thirties. I noticed myself wanting to check into a hotel the night before my birthday so I could wake up on my birthday and eat room service. The only thing better than delicious food is delicious food brought to me in bed.

This started to spill over into my regular life. Sometimes I was hungry but didn't feel like sitting upright in the restaurant. This has caused my husband much pain and anguish. He is a man who prefers his food hot and less than three minutes away from the kitchen where it was made. Bless his heart, he married a woman who wants to see how restaurants will figure out how to package sushi, wood-fired pizza, or brownies a la mode that they might be eaten in my home.

This is how I know he loves me, based on the number of times he has navigated street parking, negotiated with a valet, trekked into a restaurant, just to pick up hot food and eat it warm or have to heat it in the microwave or oven by the time he got it home, while I enjoy the thrill of having to change from my daytime pajamas to my nighttime pajamas because I accidentally drizzled eel sauce or garlic aioli on my inside clothes.

Desserts

I love desserts of all kinds! (Okay, most kinds. Bread pudding can kick rocks.) If I could receive all nutrients from desserts, I would. I would like to have a harem of desserts available to me at my beck and call.

When I was a work-study student in college I worked for the Office of the President. Our then–college president, Dr. Audrey Forbes Manley, was the first alumna president of Spelman College and had achieved a storied career as a medical doctor and worked in the surgeon general's office prior to her time as college president. She was a classy lady, the kind of woman who made you straighten your spine when she walked into a room.

One year, Dr. Manley wanted to celebrate her staff and took us to Canoe, a fancy restaurant in Atlanta, situated on a river. We were all so excited to be in such a fancy place while also trying to pretend we went to fancy places all the time.

The waiter went around the table and took our orders as Dr. Manley encouraged us to order whatever we'd like for lunch. Mrs. Mencer, the receptionist, asked for the dessert menu. A hush fell over the table. Maybe she was ordering for later? Maybe she was going to decide what to order for lunch based on what she knew she wanted to order for dessert?

"I'll have this one," Mrs. Mencer said to the waiter and pointed to her selection on the dessert menu.

The rest of us nervously told the waiter our lunch orders and the table was quiet after the waiter walked away.

"What?" Mrs. Mencer said. "My dad taught me, life is short, always order dessert first. So, I did."

Mrs. Mencer went on about her business. No embarrassment. No chagrin. No concerns for how she might be viewed or judged. And when her decadent dessert showed up to the table before all our dishes, she commenced eating her dessert and enjoying every bite of it. No one corrected her. We all just watched her commit two of the worst offending etiquette sins in the South. Ordering dessert first *and* eating her food while the rest of us waited for ours.

Okay, I love dessert, but maybe not quite as much as Mrs. Mencer.

I love a crème brûlée! Ah, a chilled yet warm, rich custard, topped with torched, candied sugar. I love crème brûlée so bad, I almost added a kitchen torch to my wedding registry until my then-fiancé, now husband, reminded me of his history of setting things on fire as a child and suggested maybe this wasn't the best purchase if I wanted him to not accidentally light our home on fire.

I love a cupcake with the right ratio of moist cake to frosting. I have been known to buy myself cupcakes for no special occasion except that it's a day that ends in *y*.

I love donuts, the breakfast of desserts, the dessert of breakfast. What a wonderful, round, dunkable, fried, yeasty invention. My favorite kind of donut is a mom-and-pop donut. There are two types of mom-and-pop donut places. One is the chef-inspired donut place, where the flavors change each month or each week according to what is in season. Where spring brings a fresh strawberry glaze and summer brings a peach fritter. The second is the kind of donut place where you could go there every day for thirty years, where the donut flavors never change and you know you can count on it. The same fritter, long john, old-fashioned donut with drip coffee with one or two options of milk you can pour in your coffee yourself because this place refuses to serve a latte.

The only national chain I will give a pass to is Krispy Kreme. This twenty-four-hour donut spot with its HOT DOUGHNUTS NOW sign is truly the stuff of dreams. This fried pillow of lightness and perfection is delicious and dangerous. With any other dozen of donuts, you would realize as your stomach tightens you cannot indeed eat the whole dozen, but after six Krispy Kremes your deceived stomach would feel like you could in fact tackle the whole dozen by yourself with no assistance. Catching the HOT DOUGHNUTS NOW sign is the equivalent of your partner stepping sexily downstairs in an outfit of silk, leather, and lingerie and letting you know it's go time. You don't think. You don't contemplate logistics. You follow the sign and ask questions later. Hot Krispy Kreme donuts are somehow a blessing and a sin, and I would like to experience both sides of that, please and thank you.

I love a good peach cobbler. Not that biscuit-covered cobbler you saw on someone's random food blog. I'm talking about tender peaches in a sweet, slightly thick syrup with a flaky, tender crust. I'm talking about equal parts crust and equal parts peaches. *A la mode.*

And speaking of a la mode. I want warm cookies *a la mode*, brownies *a la mode*, warm pie and cobbler *a la mode*. My husband *a la mode. I want a life a la mode.*

Sustaining a long-term relationship takes time, curiosity, and creativity. You have to make time to continue getting to know one another. Spending time together. Carving out a routine but not being so tethered to it that you're not willing to experiment. I love this about food. Ever since we started going together, food always switches up. Inviting me to new restaurant openings. Taking me to hole-in-the-wall places that serve delicious sandwiches, tacos, and wings. Introducing me to friends and reconnecting me with family who can cook. Always bringing the juice, the sauce, showing me tenderness, warmth, and being cool. Food reminds me to experience pleasure, to broaden my palate, to never travel to a new city just to eat from a national food chain I could eat at back home. I love food. Me and food go together real bad and we're never breaking up.

BAKING CAKES AND MAKING MAGIC

The year I turned thirty-five I received the pinnacle gift a Southern woman can receive. My mother-in-law gifted me a red KitchenAid stand mixer. This is how I knew I'd made it into the famed halls of domesticity. It didn't matter when or how often I planned to use the thing. The entire purpose of having a KitchenAid stand mixer is to stunt, to flex, to elicit jealous and covetous feelings in the hearts of others when they walk into your kitchen and realize you've made it. You've got your own house now. You've got a half bath just for guests, and you've got your very own KitchenAid stand mixer.

For months I stared at it. Marveled at its roundness. Wondered how the hell it worked and then it dawned on me: My grandma had taught me all her signature dishes except her cakes. I needed to learn how to bake a cake, a layer cake specifically, my grandmother's cake.

When I was growing up, my Grandma Bert lived in a three-bedroom, one-bathroom apartment. It was the place we gathered for Christmas, summers, and birthdays. When it was your birthday, my grandma let you pick the kind of cake. She'd make pineapple cake, German chocolate cake, coconut cake, or chocolate cake.

My favorite was chocolate cake, and by that I mean yellow cake with chocolate frosting, which is how my grandmother defined it. I would tell Grandma which cake I wanted and while she went to work in the kitchen I went outside to play. I never bothered to watch what she was doing. I assumed she gathered the flour, clapped it in her hands like LeBron James before a basketball game, spun in a circle, sprinkled glitter, and magically transformed all those ingredients into a cake. I had been to her home many times when it seemed like she didn't have much in her refrigerator or her cabinets, but by the time I came back inside there was a feast of fried chicken, greens, biscuits, and cake.

After the meal, my grandma would take the leftover fried chicken and set it to the side. She'd take the leftover cake and slice it, wrapping each slice in wax paper and taping it closed. She'd take an empty shoebox, fill it with paper towels and one side with fried chicken and the other side with cake slices. Each family would get their own shoebox to take home. About an hour into our journey in the car, on the train, on the bus, we'd lift the lid of that shoebox, and it felt like heaven was singing back to us. The glorious taste of Grandma's cake, nestled in a shoebox next to the fried chicken. How delicious and fresh everything still tasted even hours into the ride back home.

It was my thirty-fifth birthday, and I wanted to learn this

magic my grandma used to make her cakes. I wanted to know how much glitter and how long to spin in a circle. I called my grandma to get the scoop.

"Grandma, this year for my birthday I want you to help me break in my KitchenAid mixer. You've taught me how to cook everything else except I haven't learned how to make your cakes. Let's make a cake together!"

"Okay, baby, let me check my schedule," she said.

"Grandma, but you're retired. Like, do I need to call your secretary?"

"Let me check my schedule and I'll let you know," she said and changed the subject.

A week went by. I called again.

"Grandma, my birthday is coming up. I want you to teach me how to make your cakes."

"Mena, I'm not even sure I remember how to make those cakes anymore. That was so long ago," she said, changed the subject, and then rushed me off the phone.

Another week went by. I called her. Again.

"Grandma, like my birthday is coming up soooooon. Please come to my house and teach me how to make your cakes."

She paused.

"Mena, I gotta tell you something. I know you think I made those cakes from scratch . . ."

Her voice trailed off and all I could hear was the deflating sound of my childhood memories.

"But I made those cakes from a box mix, Mena."

I clutched my nonexistent pearls. *No, no, no, no. Not my grandma. My grandma gets the eggs straight from the chicken coop. My grandma threshes the wheat herself. My grandma claps the flour in the air better than LeBron James. My grandma spins in a circle and sprinkles glitter all over the place.*

She told me of a church mother who convinced her when

she was young and overwhelmed with the domestic tasks of church and home that there was no reason to keep baking cakes from scratch. *They have box mixes for that now, but how you trick 'em is by always making your frosting from scratch*, the old church mother said. So that's what my grandma did, and for years, for decades, she fooled a whole family of us.

"I don't even remember if they still make that mix I used to use," she said.

While she was trying to remember, I started googling small-batch cake mixes to see if Williams Sonoma might have stock of this rare box cake mix my grandmother used.

"It was called supamoaih."

"Grandma, what are you saying?"

"It was called supamoaih."

Anytime you have a Southern relative you have to expect some consonants to go missing when they speak to you. It's not because your cell reception is bad. It's not because you didn't hear them clearly. It's because they are from the South and consonants go missing in Southern speech all the time.

"Wait, Grandma, say it again."

"MENA. You spell it S-U-P-E-R M-O-I-S-T. Supamoaih."

It is this moment when I realize my grandma's small-batch, rare cake mix is indeed Betty Crocker's Super Moist. I want to explain to her that Betty Crocker's Super Moist cake mix will probably never go away. I want to tell her I know she doesn't watch *The Walking Dead*, but if she did, she'd know when they beat the zombies and break into the abandoned grocery store to find food for the rogue community of survivors, Betty Crocker's Super Moist will be right there on the shelf. Super Moist cake mix will survive the zombie apocalypse. I want to tell her you can go to just about any gas station convenience store in the most rural town in America and probably find Betty Crocker's Super Moist staring right at you from the aisle. I wanted to tell her, *Grandma, they are never going to stop making Super Moist!*

But I didn't say these things. Instead, I said, "It's okay, Grandma, please come to my house. We'll find a from-scratch recipe and try out my mixer for my birthday."

She agreed and we worked our way through a recipe as close to her pineapple cake as I could find. When we got into the kitchen together, she remembered. How to softly place the cake layers in your hand when transferring from the cake pan. How to mix the pineapple sauce for the middle layer. How to poke holes in the bottom layer so the pineapple sauce will seep into it, just so. She showed me how to make egg white frosting and smiled at me as I frosted the cake in the ugly way a baking beginner would.

A couple of years later, her eighty-fifth birthday was coming up. My cousin had organized a summer family beach vacation, and my grandma let us know in no uncertain terms that her birthday was to be celebrated during the beach trip while everyone was together. She had no concerns her birthday wasn't in the summer at all.

Our family came together and cooked the soul food my grandma would normally have cooked for us. I slid my hips next to my grandma and asked her what kind of cake she wanted.

"You know I want yellow cake with chocolate frosting," she said.

I baked her a Super Moist yellow cake, still doubting that she had really been baking with cake mix my whole childhood. I made the chocolate frosting from scratch just how she taught me. I tasted a little of the cake, hoping maybe I wouldn't recognize the taste. Maybe she only baked with a cake mix for the younger grandchildren. Surely, she baked from scratch for me. No. That cake tasted exactly like my childhood.

We sang "Happy Birthday" and looked around at four generations of our family. We asked Grandma to tell us stories and asked her as many questions as we could think of about when she was born and how she grew up and what she remembered of her parents and her upbringing.

"Grandma, why did you always put fried chicken and cake in that shoebox?" I asked her.

"Oh, I did that because that's what my parents did for me whenever we took a trip. We packed food during segregation in case there wasn't anyplace safe to stop along the way. I did it for my children during Jim Crow in case there wasn't a safe place to stop. I did it for you grandchildren, hoping and praying you would arrive home safe too."

My grandma's magic transcended the kitchen. She took injustice, racism, and a painful history, transforming it by mixing in love and pouring in prayers all over the place. She started a tradition I hoped to keep.

The next day a couple of my cousins had to leave early and head back to work. I wrapped some slices of cake in wax paper the same way my grandma had for us. All these years later, I still have my KitchenAid stand mixer. I still make my frosting from scratch. And I'll always be grateful for my grandma's magic and for a vintage, small-batch, rare-to-find cake mix called Betty Crocker's Super Moist.

PART 3

A LOVE LETTER TO BACK FAT, LOOSE TIDDIES, AND COMING HOME TO YOURSELF

POOL PARTIES, BIKINIS, AND PUMPS AND A BUMP

When I was growing up, we went to the pool in our apartment complex. My mom in her sleek black one-piece bathing suit; and eight-year-old me in a purple-and-pink swimsuit that looked like a fish. I got in the water. I played with my friends. Until I swam too deep for my britches and nearly lost my lungs' ability to lung in the deep end of the pool.

After that I spent summers at my dad and stepmother's house in Nebraska. My dad and stepmother were so determined for my brother Robert and me to not stay cooped up in the house all summer that they forced us to play outside for the exact amount of time we wanted to watch TV. You have never seen two children doing math as quickly as my brother and I did that summer. I wanted to watch the Michael Keaton Batman movie with the Prince soundtrack on TNT that night, which meant my brother and I needed to play outside approximately 124 minutes.

Then, my dad and stepmother decided this wasn't enough; my brother and I needed to make some friends. They told us we couldn't come back inside until we met a new friend. We walked the neighborhood, spying for kids playing in their yard. We checked every park until I met a nice white girl named Hayley. We played outside with her and her sister and had a good time until my brother got bored that we were doing "girl stuff" and went home.

Hayley and I became such good friends that she invited me to swim in the pool at her house. I asked my dad and stepmother, and they looked excited that I'd be out of the house, I mean that I met a new friend. They didn't meet Hayley's parents or do a walkthrough of Hayley's home. No! This was the eighties, when our parents had the co-parents of television, playing outside, and somebody's random house you could go to.

Having been previously mother to only a son, my stepmother relished in all the girly things she could do with me, especially my hair. She washed and deep conditioned my hair with some combination of Queen Helene's Cholesterol Hair Treatment and Straight Arrow's Mane 'n Tail. Then she'd blow-dry and straighten my hair, curling it up so pretty I felt like every week was Easter. When Hayley and I played outside I could run my fingers through my hair the same way she could run her fingers through hers.

My stepmother warned me not to dunk my head underwater, but there was no chance I'd do this. I didn't know how to swim, so I intended to just hang out in the pool with Hayley and her sister. My stepmother brushed my hair back into a bun, with a black-and-gold metallic scrunchy. She helped me pack a bag of clothes to change into and anything else she could think of I might need, and I walked up the street to Hayley's house.

When I got there, Hayley gave me the tour of her parents' split-level home. It had blue carpets and a spacious basement, and she and her sister had nice bedrooms. Then she took me to the backyard, where the family had an aboveground pool. I'd never seen such a thing! A pool! Aboveground! Wow!

We changed our clothes and got in the pool, laughing, giggling, playing, until Hayley and her sister got looks of fright on their faces and they were pointing directly behind me. I looked and screamed! It looked like a scary frog had joined us in the pool! By the looks of it, it had to be a poisonous one! Hayley's sister was bold enough to poke at it with a pool toy, and this is when we discovered this scary, poisonous frog was my black-and-gold metallic scrunchy in disguise. I reached for my bun that must have unraveled into a long, straight, curly ponytail and discovered with horror my hair had betrayed me. All of our giggling and splashing around had been just enough water for my hair to shrink back to its regular state of kinks and nappiness. I couldn't even gather enough of my hair to fit in that damn scrunchy.

I pulled my hair back as best I could and we played awhile longer. Hayley and her sister made no comment about my having a hair catastrophe, outside of a few intriguing looks they gave me and my hair, possibly pondering how had they seen my hair in two different states in one visit. Hayley's mom offered for me to stay for dinner, but I knew better. I needed to head back to my dad and stepmother's house right then.

"Mena!" my stepmother exclaimed when she saw my hair looking like a kinkback instead of a slick back.

She immediately went to work, washing out the chlorine, starting my hair routine all over again. This was not without admonishment.

"I told you not to go underwater!" she said as she greased my scalp after washing my hair.

"I didn't!" I said. "We were just playing."

I never told her how my hair and my cute scrunchy embarrassed me. But she didn't say anything else. It was like we had an unspoken understanding, sometimes these things happened. Sometimes a Black girl could be having fun, enjoying her life, and rain or a pool or the right amount of sweat could ruin her press and curl. This was a part of our Black girl life, and her silence let me know I wasn't alone in that.

After this, I mostly stayed away from pools. They just didn't seem like they brought me anything good. But by the time I became a teenager and became a part of the youth group at the church my mom joined, I had to reevaluate my stance. One of our major youth group activities was going to a water park in San Antonio called Schlitterbahn. Everyone looked forward to this! Parents looked forward to having their sullen and stinky teenagers out of their house for hours and teenagers looked forward to kiki-ing with their friends and riding every waterslide time would allow.

In my church youth group, there were rules about swimwear. Girls were expected to wear T-shirts over their swimsuits and were requested to wear one-piece suits instead of bikinis. I'd never been around these kinds of rules, but I followed suit (see what I did there!) so I'd fit in with the other church kids. I was flabbergasted to discover there were no such rules for the boys. They could show their chests and torsos all over Schlitterbahn. I wanted to complain about this, but this boy Marquez came to the water park as a guest of another boy in our youth group, and after letting my eyes glance over his pectorals and abs I decided a chest like that needs sunshine. I was totally okay with Marquez not following the rules given to the girls.

For all of my teens and into my time in college I never wore a bathing suit without a large T-shirt covering it. I'd only seen adult pool parties on TV and in music videos. While watching MC Hammer's "Pumps and a Bump" music video after school, I learned not only was Hammer 2 Legit 2 Quit but so was his animal-print Speedo and the contents it contained. This was an issue of can't touch this but also a moment of wasn't ready to see this as Hammer continued to dance, rap, and do deep body rolls. Through this educational content I learned high heels and a bikini would be important should I ever be invited to a pool party for grown folks. MC Hammer also showed us an early version of a party bus with a commandeered Oakland city bus that would transport all of the pumps and all of the bumps to said pool party.

In their music video for "Rump Shaker," Wreckx-n-Effect educated me that zooms, booms, and rumps were what I could expect at a pool party for grown people. I wasn't sure I had a rump. I wasn't sure I could shake it. I wasn't ready to zoom or boom, but the people in the music video looked like they were having a good time in their bikinis, fitted baseball hats, bandanas, and swimming trunks, especially the one Black woman playing saxophone on the beach in her bikini (shoutout to now film producer and wife of Bobby Brown, Alicia Etheredge-Brown).

I was grown enough to pay taxes by the time I went to my first adult pool party, a birthday party for deejay and actor George 2.0, who is also a founding member of the Wondaland Arts Society, the artist collective that brought us genre-bending multi-hyphenate artist Janelle Monáe.

This was a very particular era of Atlanta. In my mid- to late twenties, I had taken up the side hustle of covering Atlanta's soul music scene as a freelance journalist writing for local and regional publications, finding a place where my love of music and my love of writing could intersect. My time as a journalist led me to interviewing Janelle Monáe at the groundswell of their time as an independent artist and their transition to becoming a major label artist, writing an article about them for my first cover story. I also attended Spelman at the same time that George 2.0, Chuck Lightning, and Nate Wonder, who were also Wondaland cofounders and co-conspirators, attended Morehouse. In college, I went to a writing workshop curated by Chuck Lightning and I'd sat with friends in a dorm staircase and listened to Nate Wonder and his then–singing group croon beautiful tunes enhanced only by the stairwell echo.

Wondaland during this time in Atlanta was comprised of Black music artists, creatives, and different iterations of bands and duos. It was also a gathering place for the rest of us, graduates from the Atlanta University Center, writers, musicians, visual artists, creative and funky people who were still trying to find our place in the world, who were working day gigs to fund our nightlife of pursuing our art.

The artists in Wondaland would sometimes host events for the creative community surrounding the Wondaland Arts Society. Sometimes we read books and discussed them in a Harlem Renaissance–style salon. Sometimes we had intellectual conversations about art. Sometimes members of Wondaland would play new music and we'd vibe to it. Sometimes we'd play music real loud and dance until we were tired.

Wondaland was building and growing into music production, film, and anything else creative they could get their hands on. Those of us who were in their periphery wanted to see them succeed, wanted to see them fly, wanted to see them make it. When Wondaland got a win, it felt like we were winning too. Which is why when several of us received a late-night text that we were needed to be extras in Janelle's music video for her next song, "Tightrope," we jumped at the chance.

The women were instructed to dress in the style of Audrey Hepburn: black turtleneck, black leggings, and black shoes. The men were instructed to wear white button-down shirts, black slacks, and black shoes. If you look closely in the music video you can catch me and my teeny-weeny afro dancing next to Janelle as a part of the crew. I use the term *dancing* here very loosely. That spring, Janelle released her first album, *The Arch-Android,* on a major label, which we celebrated with her and the Wondaland team by dancing and throwing 'bows to Outkast's "Bombs Over Baghdad" in a ballroom after her album release event.

By the time the heat of an ATL summer was just reaching its peak, there was much to celebrate, so the Wondaland crew and community gathered to pool party in honor of George 2.0's birthday, held at the clubhouse of a subdivision where the crew used to hang out. The air among us felt electric with possibility. Our friends' dreams were coming true, and their hard work was paying off. It was the homie George's birthday and what better way to celebrate than a midsummer pool kickback. When I received this invitation, I assumed the goal was mainly to look cute to hang out around the pool. I wore a yellow matching tank top and wide leg pants so I could at least pull up my pants legs and put my feet in the water.

My yellow outfit and I got there a bit late, and the scene was not completely like what I envisioned on TV. People were actually in the pool, playing volleyball and chillin'. I was one of two people who didn't have on an actual swimsuit. This was the most skin I'd ever seen in real life. My sheltered church girl upbringing was coming back to bite me again.

Act normal, I told myself. *People wear bikinis and swim trunks all the time,* I told myself. But the men's bodies put Marquez's little body to shame, and these were grown women's curves in these bikinis. I received compliments on my outfit, but the assumption was that I had a swimsuit underneath. My friends were waiting for me to get in the pool, and I had no intention of doing any such thing. I didn't even own a swimsuit at the time.

I sat on the edge of the pool and put my legs in the water so I could at least talk to my friends who were frolicking in the pool. My homeboy Adán sat next to me at the pool's edge in his signature rolled cuff jeans. He was the only other person who wasn't dressed in swimwear. We sat in silence, watching everybody have a good time.

"So, this is my first grown-up pool party," I confessed.

"Word?" he said.

"Yeah, and I feel . . . overdressed," I said.

I told him about my youth group T-shirt swimwear situation, and we had a good laugh.

"I had no intentions of getting in the pool, which is why I wore these jeans," he said.

Solidarity.

Years later I was forced to buy a bikini in order to complete my last-ditch efforts at auditioning for *America's Next Top Model*. Bikini photos were required, so I bought the cutest one I could find, brown and white tiger stripes with magenta straps. My best friend took a full-length picture of me in my bikini to submit to the show. I wasn't cast for the show, but I showed a couple of friends my bikini photos and their compliments boosted my confidence. Maybe they could see me differently than I saw myself.

I wore that same bikini on my honeymoon after my husband and I got married. I also wore this same bikini on a family trip to the beach where a strong wave came and gave my cousins and my aunt more of a look at my tiddies than they'd ever asked for.

There are so many other garments that arrive with a rite of

passage: a first bra, first lingerie, first pairs of matching crew socks I wore in the 1990s. My swimwear deserved a better rite of passage. A chance to shop without carrying shame with me. An opportunity to strut my bikini or tankini or one-piece stuff around a pool or a beach anytime I wanted.

The last time my husband and I went to the beach I wore my new leopard-print two-piece and asked him to take a picture. He grabbed his phone as quickly as gravity would allow and took a picture for me to keep and for him to save. When I looked at myself in the photo, I thought my teenage youth-group self would be so astounded. *You got breasts and you showing 'em off!* she'd probably exclaim. *You fine!* But she would probably pronounce it *foin* as the singer Monica's pronunciation taught her to do.

I'm still learning my way around the pool, and I have mostly decided I am not a person who wants to be *in* the pool. My journey to the pool and the pool party has been fraught with mishaps but also includes some of the coolest moments in my life. Anyway, no more T-shirts covering up my swimsuit for me. But I did make sure to purchase a secure bikini top so I don't have any more tiddy mishaps.

MY JOURNEY TO BIG TIDDIES

n fifth grade I started to notice them: breasts. Not mine because I had a chest as flat as the notebooks I loved to write my poems in, but fifth grade was the year a few girls in class started to have *whispers* *breasts*. They had never mattered really. I had never noticed anything about them and now suddenly, they were everywhere.

This was around the era I read *Are You There God? It's Me, Margaret*. Shoutout to Judy Blume. My friends and I were sneaking into the library. We could not believe this book was there talking about training bras and periods, which was stuff we really wanted to know something about. This is what it was like to grow up without the internet. You had to go to a library and look through the Dewey decimal system to find a book that had this information. The closest we had to anything that was like a chat room where we could talk to other girls our same age was reading Judy Blume's book in the voice of this twelve-year-old girl, Margaret.

Training bras were becoming very popular. My first instance of noticing training bras was in gym class. I remember being in the locker room and everyone trying not to be looked at, and at the same time also trying not to look or trying not to be seen looking. Everyone turned and saw our classmate Shannon was wearing this glistening white training bra. It seemed to glow against her dark skin. Everyone oohed and ahhed over her training bra, and we couldn't wait to find out how she obtained such a thing. She said her mom had bought her this training bra at a department store. Her training bra had a little pink rose, placed delicately between the two cups. It was as cute and dainty as it could be. I looked at Shannon's training bra and knew I wanted one.

My friends and I were talking a lot about breasts. There was a lot of concern as to how we could get breasts more quickly because there was only a small number of girls who had breasts that were developing at that point. Most of us had not started developing and really were looking forward to having these breasts.

Between Shannon's testimonial and reading Margaret's experiences with training bras, I started to reconsider my methods. With my Pentecostal, charismatic church upbringing, I wondered if maybe I needed to wear the bra by faith. Maybe I could wear the bra for the tiddies I wanted.

I also thought praying might help. I prayed and asked God to give me a C cup because I felt this was an average ask. I'm a classic oldest kid, never asking for too much, trying to find a middle ground of things to request. The C cup felt like a moderate prayer request.

But my grandma had already prayer blocked me. My grandma is the Queen of the Big Tiddies. A buxom, petite woman—a

Coke bottle did not do justice to how I remembered her body as a child. She always told us girls in the family she prayed no one in the family would have breasts the size of hers. When I heard her say that I felt like her prayer was canceling out my prayers. If God was going to choose to answer the prayers of one of us, surely God was going to choose my grandma based on seniority and the fact that she'd been with the company longer.

I went home that day determined to get a training bra, because clearly that's what my breasts were missing: *training*. If I had had today's technology availed to me, I would have presented my mom with a PowerPoint presentation on The Importance of Amena Receiving a Training Bra: Because Otherwise How Would Her Breasts Know to Grow. But I had no such technology in the early 1990s, so I told my mom what I'm sure was a sweaty, long-winded, breathless, prepubescent story about why *we* needed to head down to the nearest department store and get *me* a training bra *stat*.

What I Remember Probably Happened:

My mother looked at my chest and then back at my face and said, "No, I'm not getting you a training bra."

What May Have Actually Happened:

My single mother looked at her tight budget and then back at my face and said, "No, I'm not getting you a training bra."

What Actually Happened:

My mother said, "No, I'm not getting you a training bra." My mom and I recently talked about this. She said her main concern wasn't just that I didn't have breasts yet, but she felt like I was still a little girl. She wanted me to be able to enjoy my time as a little girl and not transition too quickly into the age I might be where I would need a bra. Now as an adult woman, I can see my mom's perspective, but as a preteen I was not in agreement.

So, I decided to cut one of my cotton camisoles as close to the length of a bra as I could, and my mother looked at the cut camisole she'd spent her good money on and looked at my face. I decided maybe I'd wait and grow some breasts before I asked about a training bra again.

At this era of prepubescence, I was one of the tallest girls in my class. I was just arms and legs, lanky limbs all over the place. My body shape felt rectangular. I didn't really have curves in any way. I wasn't sure I had a feminine body, because at that time, I defined a feminine body as Jessica Rabbit. Is it a bad thing that my entire body image rested on a fictional cartoon character? These are questions to consider in therapy.

I was a tall and lanky eleven-year-old just at the cusp of realizing the boys who had been so gross to me were now starting to look kind of cute to me. I figured from watching television I needed these breasts to snag a boy, to be considered beautiful or attractive. Towering over my whole class did not seem to be helping me in either department. My mom continued to buy me camisoles or undershirts to wear under things, but no bras, no training.

My sixth-grade year was a time of huge transition. My mom reenlisted in the military to work as a nurse, and over Christmas break, we moved from Maryland to Texas. I moved away from my best friend and a school I loved. There was a certain kind of invisibility to moving in the middle of Christmas break. I felt like I was moving in the quiet of night because everyone was with their families doing holiday things and there was no good way for me to say goodbye. Life and my body were changing so quickly.

In Maryland, sixth grade was middle school with lockers and block scheduling. In my new home city of San Antonio, sixth grade was elementary school with cubicles and snack time. Somehow my school experience made me feel like I had gone back in time, while my body kept developing forward. I was the awkward girl with no friends, mostly because I told my classmates the only reason they liked Texas was because they hadn't been anywhere else, and they weren't as well traveled as me. If you were looking for tips on making friends, this type of attitude will certainly help!

I was used to the other kids looking at me as if I was strange, but as sixth grade wore on, I noticed a different kind of look and felt a different type of strange. Two boys turned around in my science class and I saw them looking at my chest. They whispered among themselves and laughed. My face felt hot with embarrassment. It was the first time I felt ashamed of the very body part I wanted so desperately. That summer, my mom finally bought me a bra, a real one. I didn't need training.

I was proud of that bra, and I was somehow proud of and embarrassed by my breasts. The summer before seventh grade, we went to visit my grandma and great-grandma. Nothing like seeing your extended family when you're going through puberty. It's apparent to them you are no longer the cute and cuddly kid they remembered. But you are still far from when they might view you as an adult (which could be anywhere between twenty and sixty-six years old).

My grandma had moved into a house next door to our cousin so she could have enough room to house and care for her parents. Her mom, my great-grandma Sudie, after years of working in a tobacco factory, had developed emphysema and was now a wheelchair user. Her ability to keep her breath whether standing up from sitting or walking from her bedroom to the living room was as if she had smoked packs of cigarettes all her life, even though she'd never smoked at all. When I was a little girl, she cooked and cleaned and spent time with me. This was my first time seeing her in a wheelchair.

My grandma wheeled Grandma Sudie into the room and

announced each of us in the family who had come to visit. I had my hair in curly braids with extensions and I was wearing a skort that I was very proud of. Grandma Sudie greeted each of us in a line and then she got to me, eyeing my newfound height and my newly developed breasts. Grandma Sudie was known for speaking her mind, and emphysema wasn't going to stop her this time. She looked at me and then looked over her shoulder at my grandma.

"Bert, where are her breasts?" she said.

I don't remember what my grandma or what anyone else in the room said. My grandma probably shooed Grandma Sudie's comment away, playfully instructing her to leave me alone. At the time I felt horribly embarrassed. Today, if I could go back and do it all over again, I'd turn to her and say, "Yes! Where are they?! I'm looking too because this is not the C cup I've been praying for!" But I didn't have it in me to say any of this, so I scowled awkwardly until Grandma wheeled Grandma Sudie further down the line. If you want to know how a seventh grader can want to melt into the cracks of the tile in the kitchen, it's that moment right there.

Not much had changed by the time I made it to high school. I spent my first two years of high school at a Christian school in uniforms. I didn't have time to pay attention to what my chest was or wasn't doing because I was too busy begging my mom to please let me go back to public school. After many presentations and dissertations from her teenage daughter, my mom let me go back to public school my junior year of high school.

Around this time my cousin Diane and her husband, Steve, had their second child, my cousin Stephanie. Cousin Diane and her family lived in San Antonio and were the only family we had there, so when she and Steve went out for the night, she asked my mom and me to babysit Stephanie and her older sister

Tabitha. My own baby sister was now four or five years old, and I had done a pretty good job of looking after her and other people's kids, so I felt well-versed in babysitting. My cousin Stephanie was a breeze, an easy baby, content to play in her playpen until she drifted off to sleep. My cousin Tabitha had been easy to babysit that evening too. We were on her turf after all, in her house, with her toys. But there came a time at night where it was bedtime for a four-year-old no matter how industrious she was.

"All right, Tabitha, let's start cleaning your toys up and getting ready for bed," I said.

Tabitha looked at me and then she looked at my mom. I could see her child eyes seeing through my well-versed babysitter experience. She recognized right then that just like her I was a child. I was fine to play with or play in front of, but if she wanted to delay her bedtime, she needed to escalate this to a supervisor. Tabitha turned away from me and twisted her shoulders to face my mom.

"Why do I have to listen to her? She doesn't even have any breasts!" Tabitha said, hands out in front of her, pleading.

I applaud Tabitha's logic. She had one lifeline to stay up later as she felt she should have, and her lifeline was to put me and my itty-bitty tiddies in their place. I can also see from her child understanding and in the genetics of our family how breast size could be equated to the size of one's authority. My grandma was one of the matriarchs with a well-endowed chest and nearly everyone we knew listened to her. Her mother, my mother, all with chest sizes that seemed to bear listening to. Cousin Tabitha basically said, "If I don't see a certain size of tiddy, then I don't need to respect you."

From my grown woman vantage point, I can see the logic and the hustle in her statement. But my teenage self felt mortified. Owned and dragged by someone who wasn't even old enough to attend kindergarten or tall enough to ride most roller coasters. All I could think was I was trying everything I could to find these breasts. I didn't know where they were. I didn't know how to get to them.

BY THE TIME I WENT TO COLLEGE I HAD SETTLED INTO AN ILL-gotten B cup. I was really an A cup but when my previous bras got too tight, I elected to promote myself to the medium tiddy committee without seeking any referrals, confirmations, or recommendations. I carried those B cups proudly through college, graduation, and into my early thirties . . . or so I thought.

Over the years I went through a bra revolution. My first bras came in a box from JCPenney, Sears, or Foley's before it became Macy's. Whew, what a way to tell my age! These boxes had band and cup sizes on the back, so you picked your size and carried your box to the cash register. By the time I was out on my own and on a shoestring entry-level-job budget, I bought my bras from Walmart. When I got promoted, I splurged on bras from Target.

In my twenties I went through a church breakup. Not a dating breakup with a boyfriend from church. This time, I broke up with my church. My now former church did not allow dating unless you were preparing to get married. I know this sounds like it doesn't make sense, because it doesn't make sense. There was no place for casual dating, which made things weird.

Because of this, I didn't date at all during college or in my early twenties. I didn't start dating as a full-fledged adult until I was in my mid-twenties after my church breakup. Not only were we being told not to date until we were ready to get married, but we were also told not to have sex until we got married. After I left the church, I decided I wanted to date, but I determined I wasn't ready to have sex. This also meant I had no concern about the look of my undergarments. I didn't have concern about anyone seeing them, because I wasn't dating, and I wasn't having sex. I was barely having a good kiss. My dates hardly saw my clavicle, not to mention my bra.

Because I left church, and I took my first ever church break where I didn't immediately go and try to find another church to go to, I just started hanging out and figuring out how to be a twenty-five-year-old who enjoys her life and isn't constantly within the rigors of church. I joined an online community of singles in Atlanta that sometimes had in-person meetups, so I was hearing about how people were handling their dates and their sex lives. From this, I gathered it was important for your underwear to match. You could be on a date, and maybe the person you're on the date with would see your underwear somehow. This was the first time I assessed my ragtag bunch of bras and underwear. I did not have any bras and panties that matched or came as a set. I may not have been ready to have sex yet, but just in case some sex or something sexy happened to happen to me, I wanted to be prepared. I was a grown woman with a grown-up job with health insurance and a 401(k). It was time for some matching underwear.

At this time, the biggest brand for grown woman underwear was Victoria's Secret. There were really two well-known brands at the time: Victoria's Secret and Frederick's. Victoria's Secret gave the vibe it was for the girl next door who wanted to be sexy sometimes for whoever she was dating. It was for the good girls who sometimes wanted to be naughty.

Frederick's was for the freaks, the people who wanted to wear vinyl and latex and animal print, the main hub for cupless bras and crotchless drawers. I wasn't ready for Frederick's, but Victoria's Secret felt sexy and somehow safe at the same time, so I figured this was my best place to venture and improve my mismatched underwear situation. I continued to collect Victoria's Secret matching bras and panties until I got engaged to my now husband in my early thirties.

My husband proposed to me on my birthday, and we decided we wanted a quick engagement because we were ready to start our lives together. We had three and a half months in between the proposal and our wedding, and one of the big rites of passage of being engaged was having a bridal shower. Growing up in church and in the South, you would typically have two types of shower. One bridal shower for your household things, this is the one for the older women in your life, your aunties, your mama, your grandmama, your mother-in-law. This was the one where they want to get you your casserole dishes or a good set of Pyrex. This was a family-friendly kind of bridal shower.

Then you would have the bridal shower that was for lingerie. These two things typically took the place of a bachelorette party, plus the type of conservative Christian I was at that time, I wouldn't even have known what to do at a bachelorette party. The church ladies gave me a bridal shower and my best friend planned a lingerie shower for my friends.

This meant I needed to get measured so people would know my sizes and what to buy if they were going to buy me actual lingerie sets. So, I went back to Victoria's Secret, since that was my old faithful. Over the years I had mainly estimated my bra size based on when or where my old bras were too tight or too loose, but I had never had the gall to be measured by a bra professional.

The Victoria's Secret bra fitter extended her tape measure underneath my breasts and around my back and then measured again around my back and at the largest point of my breasts.

"36 D," she said.

"Excuse me?!" I said as if she'd called my mama a name.

She eyed her measurements again and said, "36 D."

"No," I said.

"Yes," she said.

"No!" I said.

"You could wear 34 double D if you prefer," she said.

I stomped out of the store. All I could think was this lady is lying to me because I had been an itty-bitty tiddy girl for so long. My now husband, then fiancé, Matt, was with me in the mall, but he hadn't been in the store with me. By the time I walked up to him, I was so mad I was huffing and puffing. I had forgotten all my little girl prayers for big tiddies.

"You will not believe what this lady said to me!" I said to him.

I told him the measurement she gave me, and Matt lifted his hands in a praise to God. He was clearly not holding space for me and my dilemma. I stomped my way over to Macy's, thinking maybe there was something wrong with Victoria's Secret's measurement system. I was met with a Black woman bra fitter in Macy's. I let her know just how wrong my measurements came out at Victoria's Secret, and she nodded and chuckled and then showed me my measurements based on her tape measure.

"That's you," she said. "This is all you now."

APPARENTLY, I HAD A HORMONAL SHIFT AND GROWTH SPURT IN MY late twenties and early thirties. Somehow these breasts are even bigger than they were at that time when I got measured. This is how I arrived in the big tiddy club. I did not realize I would get to be a member of the big tiddy club, because my grandma was praying against it. And I had all those years where these were not big tiddies.

I invited a girlfriend of mine to celebrate my grandma's birthday several years ago and this was the first time in a long time that she had seen me, my mom, and my grandma in the same room. She looked at me and she said, "Why would you think that you would not have big breasts looking at your mom and your grandma? Why would you think that?"

I wanted to take her outside and ask her why she would say that to me. But then I looked at my mom and my grandma and I could see how this would be coming for me. I understood then that I come from women of the big tiddy. I come from women who are well endowed. I can see now that this might have been on its way down to me all along.

My Grandma Sudie passed away when I was in high school, so she never got to see me now. She would not have had to ask my grandma where my breasts are. A few years ago, I saw my cousin Tabitha, both of us now grown women.

"Do you remember saying to me that you didn't have to listen to me because I didn't have any breasts?" I asked her.

She shook her head. She did not remember at all.

"But now you do have to listen to me. You have to listen to every word I say," I said and poked my tiddies out.

Now my grandma and I trade bra advice and recommendations. If it's a little chilly outside, my friends ask me if I need a jacket and I tell them no because my tiddies hold heat. Most times my tiddies enter the room before I do. And like my grandma I can sometimes not see around my chest to buckle my seat belt. I have come to understand the importance of a good quality bra. Of finding the waist in every outfit, so my tiddies don't create an unwanted tent. God really did answer my tiddy prayer above all I could ask or think. I hope I always carry these thangs with pride, even if someday I have to pick them up from my knees.

NEVER TELL A BLACK GIRL HOW TO BLACK GIRL

Never tell a Black girl how to Black Girl
We Black Girl in every way we want to
With this skin and these hips
We change our hair according to our mood
We change our hair just to keep them fooled

We moisturize
We side-eye
We sit between each other's legs and grease each other's
    scalps
Turn our kitchen into a salon
Turn sidewalks into a runway
We take up space and will not apologize
    for it

We double Dutch
We "Miss Mary Mac all dressed in black"
We "let's get the rhythm of the hands"
We "me and you us never part"

We move our hips to hip hop
We head bang to heavy metal
We hit the Quan
We dutty wine
We waltz, salsa, rumba, merengue
We electric slide
Every time we dance, we reclaim our time

We pray
We asé
We practice yoga
We meditate
We call on Jesus
We pray to Allah
We wear hijab
Some of us prefer not to call on a god at all

We hood
We suburban
We country
We urban
We global

We scientist
We physicist
We work behind the scenes

Beside the scene
We build the scene
We are the scene
We start hashtags and build movements
We laugh loud and move quiet
They tried to erase us
And we still here despite it

We deserve honor
We deserve respect
We stay woke and we want our checks

We run the world Beyoncé
We Rihanna work work work
We lead the revolution and we twerk
We Sweet Honey in the Rock
We Celie and Nettie and Shug
We Women of Brewster Place
We Ntozake and Toni and Alice
We Maya and Nikki and Phyllis
We Audre and Marsha

We Shirley Chisholm
We unbought, we unbossed
We invented the juice
We created the sauce

We are Black girls who make magic
We are Black girls who rock
When we lift each other up
We cannot be stopped

Black girl
We are us
We are me and you
Never tell a Black girl how to Black Girl
We Black Girl in every way we want to

LOOK AT THAT THONG SO SCANDALOUS

t started with strings, the song and the thong. Sisqó from Dru Hill fame wrote a song that made thongs famous, the "Thong Song." It was 1999, the era of the lowest-rise jean, the kind where girls wanted their thongs to peek out above their waistline. I was a church girl then. I wore long shirts over my low-rise jeans and never wore a crop top until I was in my thirties. At the time, I was more concerned with words like *modesty, purity, pantyhose,* and *slips.*

My best friend Adrienne and I had known each other since high school, growing up in San Antonio, Texas. She went to college near Dallas, and I went to college in Atlanta. We always met up to hang out when we returned home for school breaks. Around our sophomore year of college, we were starting to interview for internships and summer jobs where we would need to wear business attire.

Because I liked to be studious in all areas of life, I even attended mock interviews hosted by a corporation that partnered with Spelman at the time. We dressed up in suits and dresses as if the interview were real, completed the interview, and then the HR professionals would give us feedback to help us in our future real interviews. Leaving this interview, one of the students who was a year or two older than me got in her car, turned up the "Thong Song," and bounced in her blazer all the way out of the parking lot.

I could not understand how such a small set of underwear could be that inspiring, until the summer between sophomore and junior years of college. My friends from college had started talking about panty lines, how they weren't supposed to show, especially in office attire, and how wearing a thong could be a solution. Adrienne and I were out shopping and came across a bargain bin full of thongs. These could solve all our dress pant panty line problems.

In an era where we still shopped at The Limited and wide-leg dress pants were in, the logic seemed simple enough. So, she bought one and I bought one too. After we finished shopping, I went home to drop my bags off to go back out and hang with my friends. When I got home later that night the bag with the thong wasn't where I'd left it. I was looking all over the house for it when my mom came out of her room with the shopping bag clutched in her fist.

"What you need this for? Who you wearing this for?" she said as if she were cross-examining a guilty defendant.

"I wanna be prepared for job interviews and business attire. I don't want my panty line to show," I said, voice trembling because I wasn't sure how concerned I should have been for my life at that point.

I don't remember if my mom said anything else. I just remember she went into her room and came back not with the thong I purchased but with a different pair of underwear. My mom confiscated my thong and handed me a pair of bloomers she had bought me. They had mesh on the side like a basketball jersey.

"Here, if you're worried about your panty line wear these," she said, and I never saw that thong again.

Shortly after I graduated college, I got my first professional gig performing poetry. My best friend Kimberly and another woman we went to church with took me shopping because they looked at my wardrobe (using *wardrobe* here is really generous) and told me I could not go to the gig dressed like that. They took me on a mid-budget shopping spree. We went to The Limited and Nordstrom and made it lightly drizzle, since we weren't spending enough money to make it rain. It was their treat because they knew I couldn't afford any of it. I had two events, so they bought me two outfits down to the shoes. The only thing left was underwear.

"Do you have a thong?" they asked me.

I thought about the bloomers my mom had given me years before and said no.

They marched me back into the store and bought me two thongs. The day of the gig I was *nervous as hell.* Not only was I getting paid to perform poetry for the first time, but this was my first time wearing a thong. Now I have more thong knowledge: buy the material that suits your outfit, your size, and your booty cheeks, and ensures overall comfort. But back then I didn't know anything, so I wore what I'd been given.

About an hour before I was supposed to go onstage at the venue, I had to go to the bathroom. The thong was cotton and double reinforced at the seams, which pinched me in all the wrong places. I couldn't tell if I was going to the bathroom because I had to pee or if I was going to the bathroom so I could rest my nether region for a few minutes.

I made it to the bathroom and stood in the stall for a while wondering how much surgical pain I would be in. I winced after pulling the underwear down, went to the bathroom, and then I just sat there for a while, enjoying a thong-free life until two white women I didn't know came into the bathroom.

I overheard them talking. One of them had brought the other one a pair of jeans. The other one was singing at the same event I was performing poetry at. She tried on the jeans her friend brought her.

"Do you think I can get away with going commando?" she said.

Going commando? I couldn't completely tell from the context clues, but it seemed like this had something to do with the kind of underwear you wear under your pants. If there was any alternative solution to this thong-wearing I was ready to hear it!

I decided as much as I enjoyed resting my butt and vulva, I needed to put these pinching panties on and see if I could eavesdrop any further. I walked out of the stall, and we all said hello to each other. I washed my hands and finally got up the courage.

"What's commando?" I asked them.

"Oh, that's when you don't wear underwear!" one of them said.

Her name is Candi, and that's how we met, and she is still one of my good friends to this day!

I survived the pinchy thongs for my first two professional gigs. I made a wonderful friend because I wasn't afraid to ask a stranger about underwear practices or the lack thereof. But a few more years passed before I got up the courage to buy a thong with my own money.

I went back to Victoria's Secret. I bought two lace thongs, and from there my life transformed. I had a thong; I had no panty line, and I didn't feel like my undercarriage was going to be ripped away from me.

Since then, I've learned some valuable lessons:

1. Thongs don't have to be uncomfortable.

2. Those bloomers my mom gave me were really comfortable and are now called full-coverage underwear. I purchased some of my own years later but never found that sporty mesh on the side like the ones she bought me.

3. Talking about underwear is a great way to make new friends! What. WHAT.

4. You're singing the "Thong Song," aren't you?

You're welcome.

A BODY SALUTE

A salute to the folds of fat my bra won't hide
Delicious rolls of skin
Thick and sweet like a cinnamon roll

To the pinchable haunches
The love handles
That love to peek above the waist of my jeans
And flirt with whoever passes by

To my belly
That will take a low-rise pant and give a burlesque show

To my tiddies
Who hang low
Who confuse booty music for booby music

Who hear round and round we go
And do their best to scrub the ground

To the fat underneath my arms
For my left arm gently jiggling baby
For my right arm swinging its neck and saying go 'head
    baby

To my booty for never giving up on me
For growing round, low, and full
For finally learning how to twerk something
Shake something

To the craters of cellulite
Slathered like icing on the cake of my thighs
Sponsored by cornbread and yeast rolls

To the stretch marks
That sit at the corners of my hips
Like blinking loud neon signs in front of the club that say
Here
Is where you have a good time

It is a glory
This body
Its moles
And its dry patches
Its wrinkles and scars
Its curly hairs, including the gray and silver ones
This body is a love that grows, becomes, changes
This body is me

PART 4

THE BLACK WOMEN WHO RAISED ME, CHURCH GIRL SHENANIGANS, AND THERAPY MISHAPS

UNBOUNDING

A Prayer

To the God of my great-grandmother
To the God who meets in living rooms
Who sits at the liver-spotted ankles of old Black
    women
Who finds a worship service in the songs Black women
    sing to get through the day
A field song
A deliciously dirty blues
A hymn whose words have never been written down
A jazz riff for Ella and Billie and Ma
A hum and moan
A scat that has no words at all

To the God who understands this as language
As praise
As lament
As joy mixed with cornmeal and flour and fried to crispy
    perfection

To the God who understands a braless unbounding
A place for tiddies to hang unfettered
Where concerns, hopes, and wishes hang on the line by
    clothespins
Where dreams are pressed and curled but will still rise
    defiant

To the God of Judge Wapner and *The Young and the
Restless*
Who listens to concerns for Victor and Nikki and Mrs.
    Chancellor
Who knows *The People's Court* is not always for the people

To the God who works in the storm and the rain
And the silence of unplugging damn near everything
Who keeps oil from the last fry

GRANDMA AND
HER BRA STRAPS

When my grandma talks about her husband, William, the amount of *h*'s she adds to his name in her North Carolina accent tells me how much she loved him.

"My husband, Whhhiyum, he looked just like Sidney *Pwateeyay*," she says with a little smile.

Her husband passed on long before I was born. My grandma dated but never remarried. She raised four children and by the time her five grandchildren came along, she talked to us less about relationships and marriage, and more about getting an education and finding meaningful careers. In my family, I felt more pressure to get a degree than I did to get married.

Which is why I wasn't looking for a husband when I met

my now husband, Matt. Cue the meet-cute music. We started out as just friends. We met at a church where I was performing poetry. We connected on Myspace (I just . . . if I try to explain to you . . . imagine if Facebook and Tumblr combined . . .). We met up again on Atlanta's indie artist scene and discovered we were both performers: me a poet and him a saxophone-playing deejay/music producer.

We spent two years as purely platonic friends who didn't flirt with each other or allude to being more than friends. With one catch . . . I'd had a crush on him since almost the very beginning. We worked in the studio together. We performed at events together. We built shows together. We kept coming up with excuses to see each other and finally decided to take this friendship to the next level: becoming each other's boo.

A few weeks into dating, I knew I wanted to marry him, and he told me he felt the same. We started the rounds of introducing each other to our families. This was a big deal for me. I'd never introduced any man I dated to my family on purpose. They may have come across some men I'd dated at a show here or there, but never because I intended for them to meet. When I say my family, I mean my mom, grandma, and sister. These three women are the center of my family of origin, and bringing a man home to meet them was no simple feat.

My mom raised two artistic children and wanted my sister and me to focus on developing our artist selves. My mom and grandma knew too well that life could deal you a lot of unexpected heartbreak, so they encouraged us to build lives where we retained our voice, our money, and our autonomy, where we did not build a life dependent upon a future partner. So, they knew it was serious, and I knew it was serious when I asked my mom if I could bring my boyfriend over to her house to meet them. I wasn't nervous to bring a white guy into my mother's home. I was honestly nervous to bring a man into my mom's home period. But there I was, walking into my mama's house, holding hands with my red-headed white man boyfriend.

My grandmother was sitting in the living room, and my mom and sister were busy in the kitchen. I introduced Matt to everyone and encouraged him to sit in the living room with my grandma while I helped my mom and sister finish up dinner. Just as dinner was almost ready to be served, I decided to check on Matt in the living room.

As I walked up to the couch, I noticed my grandma shrugging her shoulders and tugging at her bra straps. I immediately wondered what my grandma could be telling my boyfriend that would require her to tug on her bra straps. Turns out they were talking about swimming.

My grandma has always wanted us to learn how to swim. My mom learned but she hasn't yet been able to convince my sister and me. My grandma brings this up to every stranger and family member she can tell it to. Matt has experience as an improv performer. He is excellent at the "yes and" so he went to "yes and"-ing the hell out of my grandma.

"Man, Grandma, I love to swim! That's one of my favorite ways to exercise," he said.

"Ohhhh, I been trying to get these girls to learn how to swim. See, I would go swimming myself, but see I'm top heavy."

This is where the tugging of the bra straps came in.

"And when you're top heavy, you need a swimsuit with wide straps," she said.

"Oh, Grandma, let me know if you ever find a swimsuit you like. I'd love to take you swimming. I could teach you how to float," Matt said.

"Oh, Matt," she said, dismissing him with flirtatious fingers.

We sat down for dinner and volleyed questions and answers back and forth as they got to know Matt and Matt got to know them. My mom even waited right until we were about to leave before she asked Matt in her sternest mom voice what his intentions were with me. Matt paused at the door.

"Well," Matt said. "We're both grown and in our thirties, so my intention is to see if heading toward marriage feels right for us and if it does that's what we'd like to do."

He smiled and I did too. Okay, my mom didn't. Matt wasn't gonna get off that easy. But she let him come back to her home a few times after that, and one night after months had passed, she asked him to take a look at her carpet shampooer, and I knew Matt had the Mom seal of approval.

Months later, Matt asked me to marry him on my birthday. I said yes and we decided to have a short engagement. I spent the next three months between the church where we were getting married, running every kind of wedding errand, and going back and forth to my mom's house for emotional and wedding support. One day during this engagement frenzy, I went back to my mom's home. Grandma opened the door for me and went back to the kitchen to finish up a phone call.

When she hung up the phone, I said, "Grandma, what you been up to?"

"Oh nothing. Just telling your business," she said.

Apparently between the dinner, the proposal, and that very moment, my grandma had established her own telecommunications company with the way she was passing the word to the family. She told them not only was I engaged to this white man ("Mm-hmm yes, he's hhwhhite!") but she was sure I had found *the one* ("Yes, she held his hand right in front of us! We love him! He's wunnaful."). "Wunnaful" is the fun, Southern way my grandma says the word *wonderful*. Try it and see if it doesn't make you giggle a little bit.

"Sit down, I got something I want to tell you!" she said and sat at the dining room table.

I sat down too, awaiting what was on the other side of this urgency.

"I want you to remember, don't kiss Matt too hard," she said.

I scanned through the way I had kissed Matt recently, trying to discover if this was one of those moments where my grandma had a premonition or had otherwise discerned something I hadn't told her. Or had I, like a character in a sitcom, given Matt a hickey and didn't know it?! Then I got nervous. What was my grandma about to admit to me about her own knowledge of kissing or *whispers* sex? My nosiness got the best of me. I had to know where all of this was coming from.

"Why, Grandma?"

"Well, don't kiss Matt too hard because hhwhhite people bruise easy."

Before I could catch it, my hand clasped over my mouth. My grandma commenced to telling me how when she was working with white women, they told her they spanked their kids with wet towels so they wouldn't have bruises. It's during this part of the story I hear my mom coming down the hall and I am transported to a scene from *The Color Purple*.

This is a transcendent experience and condition that many Black women have. Sometimes it arrives in a vision. Sometimes it is an out-of-body experience where others around you continue to talk but you don't remember a word they said because you are now in the kitchen when Nettie was teaching Celie how to read. This condition can't be remedied. Once a Black woman is having a *The Color Purple* Moment, those around her have to hold space with her until the moment has passed. If another Black woman is present, she may step in and say a few lines from the movie so she can discern where in the story the other Black woman is.

In that moment, I was transported to the scene where Celie

finna shave Mister. Shug Avery is daintily painting her finger-nails in a field of purple flowers as one is wont to do. Shug re-members that not only is Celie finna shave Mister, but Celie has right and cause to kill Mister, and she also now has a weapon.

Cut to the scene where Celie is sharpening the razor and Mister is talking shit, as usual, too stupid to realize his life is hanging in the balance. *But Shug.* Shug realizes his life is hang-ing in the balance, and more than that, Celie's life is hanging in the balance. Shug forgoes her dainty manicure and begins to run back up to the house, where Celie is finna shave Mister on the porch. Cue African drums to remind us while Celie is here in America dealing with Mister's bullshit, her sister Nettie, whose letters she discovered Mister kept from her, is in Africa, learning about our people.

My mom and Shug Avery are running in lockstep. Except my mom is not trying to prevent a murder; my mom is trying to keep her mom from telling me something that neither of us can unhear.

Shug arrives breathless, but just in time to catch Celie's wrist before Celie cuts Mister clean 'cross his neck. My mom arrives to the dining room table barely catching her breath.

"Mom!" she calls to my grandma. "You don't have to worry about how hard Mena is kissing Matt. They're getting married. She can kiss him as hard as she wants to."

My grandma looks at me and then at my mom and says, "Well, she better watch it, right here," and drapes her fingers from her neck to her collarbone.

I am left to wonder: Did I leave a mark? Did I kiss my white man boyfriend too hard?

TO THIS DAY I SOMETIMES FEEL MY GRANDMOTHER LOVES MATT just a little more than she loves me. If I go out to eat and bring her some food, she wants to know, "What did you get for Matt?" If I go shopping for myself, she wants to know, "What did you buy for Matt?" If I go out of town without my husband, she wants to know, "What will Matt eat?" as if Matt has not been making food for himself all his adult years.

At one of our family beach vacations where all my grandma's kids, grandkids, and great-grandkids gathered, my grandma had finally found a wide-strapped bathing suit for herself. We gathered in a Hilton Head beach house with a pool, the TV in the living room vacillating between CNN and the tennis match. My grandmother, cousins, and husband were outside at the pool. I was in my favorite place: inside. With the air-conditioning. AC and I have had so much love for each other over the years.

Matt got out of the pool, came inside, and said, "Babe, you gotta come out here and see your grandma. Bring your phone so you can take a picture."

I step outside and see my cutie patootie grandma in the most adorable of bathing suits, wide straps and all, donning a pair of sunglasses, stepping her way into the pool.

"She said it's her first time," my cousin said.

My grandma was so happy to be in the pool she was giddy. I rewound through all the random memories I had of my grandmother putting all the grandmotherly pressure on us she could muster to learn how to swim. My grandma tugging on her bra straps while talking to my boyfriend about the swimming she'd like to do, if only she could find a bathing suit that could house all her top-heavy beauty.

She explained to us how in the North Carolina town she grew up in, the only pool was whites only. Black folks were relegated to swimming in nearby lakes or rivers, which exposed them to higher risks of injury and drowning. It was illegal for my grandmother to swim in the public pool even into her adulthood. And there she was stepping into a pool for the first time.

We marveled at our grandmother deciding a racist history didn't get to tell the end of her story, that even in her eighties she could defy history and still try new things.

We took pictures and smiled and laughed with her. Whenever Matt encouraged her from inside of the pool, she flashed her flirtatious fingers at him and said, "Oh, Matt!" I smiled, so glad to have been a witness to such a beautiful moment, and to more fully understand that my grandma would never stop flirting with my husband, even if it meant tugging on her bra straps.

HOW I BECAME A WRITER

grew up in a house full of books. My mom had a bamboo wall unit that housed rows and rows of books: Toni Morrison's *Tar Baby* and *Beloved*, Alice Walker's *The Temple of My Familiar*, books by D. H. Lawrence, books by Terry McMillan, and a book collection about figures in Black history. My mom's reading tastes were varied and curious, and new books were always being added to her library.

The books were clearly out in the open and in full view, but some of them I felt I had to sneak to read. As a little kid, I grabbed *Tar Baby* to read in my closet and put it back because even though the words were beautiful, I didn't understand any of them. In junior high, I took *Beloved* to my room but put it back after a couple of days because I couldn't tell which characters were living and which characters were dead.

As a child, I had my own collection of books: *Goodnight*

Moon, Mufaro's Beautiful Daughters, Dr. Seuss, and the Berenstain Bears. As I got older, I added Judy Blume, Beverly Cleary's *Ramona* series, and Virginia Hamilton. It was the love of reading that led me to want to be a writer.

I wrote my first poetry book in Mrs. Perry's fourth-grade class. We read some of Dr. King's speeches and then she tasked us with writing our own poetry based on how his work inspired us. I wrote a beautiful poetic treatise to Dr. King and Halloween and autumn and our school secretary and principal. As true artistes, my best friend Porsha and I took two of her mom's hand towels and used them as the cover of our newly "published" works. Mrs. Perry provided blue duct tape and stiff cardboard for the book backing and spine.

After that I started writing in notebooks, outside of class. My mom bought me my first journal, a lock-and-key Strawberry Shortcake diary. I didn't want to write my poems there, so I kept a separate steno notebook I found around the house and wrote poems in it. My mom always supported the idea of her daughters writing. She told me a woman should always have a place where she can be unedited, and she said a journal could be one of those places.

Of course, in the same breath, because this was parenting in the 1990s, she told me she didn't believe in privacy and that if she found anything I'd written in a notebook or a note I'd written to a friend in class, she was going to read it. She let me know it was her job as my mother to *know*, and how could she know if she didn't read?

Case in point, one day I came home from school and she said, "Who's Terrence?" with a carefully folded note that said "pull" on the outside squeezed between her fingers.

"Just somebody in my chemistry class," I'd said.

"I'm not sending you to school to learn *that* kind of chemistry," she said.

But when she found my first notebook of poems when I was in middle school, her words watered the seed of becoming a writer; a seed already growing in my heart.

"This is beautiful," she said, holding my notebook in her hands. "You should keep this up!"

IT MEANT THE WORLD TO ME THAT SHE THOUGHT SO. AND AT THE same time, how could I truly trust my mom as a literary critic and judge to decide my future as a writer? She thought I was brilliant when I learned how to tie my shoe the first time.

But I kept writing. Through middle school into high school, and at this point my mom decided she had a writer on her hands and it was her job as my parent to encourage me.

She took me to the library, to the government documents section, which was full of binders with pages you had to photocopy if you wanted to use them, instead of the quick visit to a .gov site and a download of a PDF this task would require today. We took all the poems I'd written up until then and filled out the paperwork to have them copyrighted. I had two volumes of poetry copyrighted before I graduated high school.

Every year, my church held an oratorical competition for Black history month, where students in elementary, middle, and high school could compete by memorizing the work of a figure in Black history or by composing your own poem or speech about Black history. I never trusted my own work, so I always memorized the work of other poets: Maya Angelou, James Weldon Johnson, or Paul Robeson. And I always got third place, to my mom's chagrin.

"Those judges don't know what they're talking about!" she'd say on the ride home. "They let that girl win because she wrote her own poem. You would have won if you had done some of your own poetry."

I didn't think my poetry was very good. I enjoyed writing it, but I had no notion that anyone else would enjoy reading or hearing my work besides my mom.

Then a beautiful year arrived: 1996. For history's sake, 1996 was the year the Fugees released *The Score*, Jay-Z dropped his debut album, *Reasonable Doubt*, Tupac bestowed upon us *All Eyez on Me*, Maxwell gifted us with *Urban Hang Suite*, De La Soul launched *Stakes Is High*, Nas composed *It Was Written*, and The Roots continued the conversation with *Illadelph Halflife*.

Kids were crowding in ciphers in the courtyard of my high school and in the parking lot at church, spitting raps and kicking freestyles. I leaned in to listen, but I was too nervous to say any rhymes until one of my friends at church invited me into the cipher. I recited Maya Angelou's "Phenomenal Woman" to the beat my friend was beatboxing. It was the only thing I could think of to perform. My friends gave me the requisite back claps of approval that I had done a good thing and that it sounded good. Then they said, "You should write some raps."

I wasn't too sure I'd have any future as a rapper, so I did what I normally do when I encounter something I'm not sure about. I researched. I turned on my alarm clock radio cassette player, listened to the radio, and every time a woman rapper came on the radio I recorded it on a cassette tape. My church boyfriend bought me a cassette single of Boss's "Deeper." My friend from church recorded a cassette of the Fugees for me and I fast-forwarded through Pras's and Wyclef's raps to get to all of Lauryn Hill's verses. I listened to Missy Elliott and Left Eye and Lady of Rage and Yo-Yo. Then I took one of my spiral notebooks my mom had originally bought for me to use for class and turned it into a rap notebook. When that notebook filled with raps, I started writing in another one. If class got boring, I wrote raps in the back of my notebook. I looked so studious in math and science class, but I was really trying to figure out what else rhymed with the word *façade.*

I came up with a rap name for myself: Teknique, inspired by Rakim's "Don't Sweat the Technique," misspelled because isn't that also hip hop?! My friends from church and I decided to form a hip hop collective similar to Wu-Tang Clan. We called ourselves Da Posse. Let's not focus on the name and get back to the story. We called each other on three-way until six of us could get on the phone. One of us would play the beat and then we'd write for a while. After that we'd spit our verses to each other and tell each other how dope we were. Then we got sophisticated. We started taking our parents' cassette tapes of sermons from church, and we recorded rap instrumentals on them so we could pass them out to each other on Sunday. Sorry, Mom.

Once I got the beat home, I'd listen to get the mood of it and then I'd turn it off and just write. When, ahem, Da Posse called for our next verse-sharing conference call I was ready to read what I thought was a pretty good rap verse. Everyone went around and read their verses, and I was last. When I finished my verse, it was kind of quiet.

"Yo, that's dope, but you can't do that, Amena," they said.

"Can't do what?" I said.

"Like it's six of us so we each only get eight bars. Your verse would be like thirty-seven bars. Did you even listen to the music to see how long your verse should be? Did you count the bars?" they said.

"Bars? What are those?" I said.

"Bars of music," they said and tried to demonstrate to me how to count the bars.

I shook my head. "I'll try to shorten it," I said.

I got my verses down to the required eight bars—most of the time. We had put together a couple of songs and a member of our group had found a studio for us to go to. Our first single was a song called "Sagginym," which is "my niggas" backward. I went to my mom, very excited about the development of our group progressing to studio time. And that was the end of my rap career.

My mom heard "my daughter," "studio," "n-word," and let me know I would be doing no such thing. No child of hers was going to be caught on wax saying the n-word, "Irregardless," she said.

"What if you become president and they look into your past and find this?" she said as my rap dreams deflated.

Mom, I hate to break it to you, but it turns out presidents can have terrible things in their past and still get elected.

The following year, a serendipitous film was released, *Love Jones*. Directed by Theodore Witcher and starring Nia Long and Larenz Tate in what started out as a beautiful romantic story and devolved into a bit of a toxic relationship. That part didn't really matter to me at the time. The part that mattered was the moment Larenz Tate stepped to the mic in a Chicago poetry lounge and spit "Brother to the Night" as his character Darius, a poem written by Regie Gibson.

The upright bass, the microphone on a stand, the saxophone, the tight rhyme scheme that led me to love hip hop, but the ability to say rhymes for as many bars as the poem decided. I didn't know to call it spoken word poetry then; all I knew was somehow I'd found a type of art that combined two things I loved: hip hop and poetry.

It didn't matter that my mom had squashed my rap career. Well, she allowed me to keep up my "Christian" rap career, where two of my friends from church and I formed a rap trio called Strange Menacetas (pronounced "Strange Ministas," a play on Strange Ministers). It was the 1990s, so spelling it with the word *menace* made so much sense at the time. At least it made sense until we started doing rap performances at other churches. Because we lived in San Antonio and kept being introduced as Strange Mena-*citas*, we could have really made a splash on the quinceañera circuit.

Other than Strange Menacetas, which could have been either a girl Christian rap trio or an opening act for a mariachi band, my mom was clear I would not have a rap career. *Love Jones* gave me hope maybe there was something else I could do with my love of hip hop and poetry. I wrote a *Love Jones*–inspired poem called "Chocolate Mista" and no you are not going to read a copy of it here. Nope. No.

But unbeknownst to me, my mom found an abandoned copy of "Chocolate Mista" sitting near the printer in our house and she had an idea. The NAACP has an annual local and national competition called ACT-SO, which stands for Afro-Academic, Cultural, Technological, and Scientific Olympics. Students competed in their local ACT-SO and if they won, they qualified to compete in the national ACT-SO competition. Still without telling me, my mom submitted "Chocolate Mista" to the ACT-SO poetry category, and it won! I found this out very casually one day after school.

My mom announced I'd won a poetry competition I had no memory of submitting a poem for. She also let me know as the winner in my category, I needed to attend the ceremony that weekend and receive my award. Then she smiled. The kind of mom smile that let me know missing this ceremony wasn't really an option, so I mumbled to myself, in my room, where she couldn't hear me, that I had no interest in going. But when the day of the awards ceremony rolled around, I got dressed and was ready just in case, because I really didn't want the other side of what could happen instead of that smile.

My mom is a cheerleader for her children until the end of time. I had a short stint as a track runner because a track coach at my new high school spotted me in a class with one of her other athletes and assumed I ran track too.

"Stand up," the coach said.

When I stood and revealed my almost six feet of height, she said, "You come out to the track too!"

So, I did. Mostly because I was scared. I casually mentioned this interaction to my mom and the next day at track practice—a track practice that was going very badly for me, a very uncoordinated, non-athletic teenager—my mom appeared in the bleachers with my little sister and proceeded to cheer for me like I must have been running in the Olympics. She did not get an athlete out of me, but it was very clear to her that her baby was a writer and maybe a little nudge would help me see it too.

To receive my winning certificate, I would be expected to read my poem in front of everyone, something I'd never done. I took my shaking page up to the podium when they called my name and read my poem. I watched adults and kids alike lean into what I was saying as if my words mattered to them. In that moment I felt something bigger than me was present in my words; there was power and connection between writing and speaking the words I was inspired to write.

That day at the ACT-SO competition, everything connected: *Love Jones*, hip hop, reading Sonia Sanchez and Nikki Giovanni, Da Posse's never-recorded rap hit "Sagginym." All these things had a place in my poems, in my writing. I wanted to be able to perform my poetry and give breath and life to the words I'd written on a page. That day I fell in love with the place where writing and performing met, and I've been performing my own work ever since.

So shoutout to my mom for being all up in my business and entering me into a competition I never would have entered myself. Shoutout to my mom for nurturing a shy, introverted kid to try speaking my words onstage. Shoutout to my mom for cheering me on, *irregardless*.

INTERNATIONAL BLACK GIRL HEADQUARTERS

n the late 1990s I moved into my dorm in Atlanta at Spelman College, sight unseen. I didn't tour the college and had barely been to the city prior to my first year of school. It was the tail end of a hot and muggy Georgia summer, with heat, humidity, and the sounds of Outkast's *Aquemini* and Lauryn Hill's *The Miseducation* wafting out of every car and dorm room window.

My mom and a family friend helped me move in, and I stood on the sidewalk in front of my dorm on my mom's last day in the city after multiple trips to Walmart and Bed Bath & Beyond. I hugged my mom. Was either of us ready for this? We weren't sure. But we had to try. She'd raised me for this. A single mom. A military veteran. She had showed me how to roll my clothes when I packed them to make more room. Our military life had given me the skill of being able to make friends just about anywhere. We said goodbye. I promised to call. As she headed to the airport I settled in with my new roommates: Erika from Washington State, Marissa from the Virgin Islands, and Shayla from upstate New York.

The first week of student orientation we were sequestered behind the gates of Spelman, learning sisterhood cheers, chants, and songs; memorizing the Spelman hymn; and acquainting ourselves with campus. Student orientation week culminated in an annual Atlanta University Center event, Olive Branch. All six AUC schools—Clark Atlanta University, Interdenominational Theological Center, Morehouse College, Morehouse School of Medicine, Morris Brown College, and Spelman—gathered for a student symposium. Every student wore the same Olive Branch T-shirt, which featured the logos of all six schools, which meant for the most part we couldn't tell who went to what school. We were all attending separate schools, but we were all also having many of the same experiences. The speakers and other students ahead of us reminded us we were one, and this thought ushered us into our first year of college or first year of postgrad.

Olive Branch culminated in a block party for the undergrad students, and each year the location rotated between the four undergrad campuses. My first year the block party was held at Spelman in what is now the amphitheater. A deejay was spinning all our favorite tunes from high school, and it was the first time all the students from all the AUC undergrad schools had the opportunity to intermingle. Meaning, some Spelman students had been sequestered away from boys and men for an entire seven days except for the periodic BellSouth man who had to enter the dorm to connect our telephone lines. *Man on the hall.* While some Spelman students were experiencing a type of wonderland where they could survey the options of who they might be attracted to.

All students were supposed to keep their Olive Branch

shirts on, but after the student symposium this didn't last long. When my roommates and I showed up to the block party, T-shirts be damned. There were tank tops and tube tops and sleeveless T-shirts intended to show off cleavage and muscles depending on the individual.

I too wanted an opportunity to show off my individualism and style. I also wanted the opportunity to don a new self. Not the awkward church girl. Not the girl who was the star in her own sitcom called *Black Girl Who Doesn't Know Things*. I wanted to be fly, sexy, attractive. I wanted to create a new me and maybe Olive Branch was the time to do it.

I went back to my dorm, Manley Hall, wearing my flare leg ombre blue jeans, and tied my Olive Branch T-shirt in a knot at my waist, hoping to show off my slight hips and A-cup chest that desperately wanted to be a B cup. I found my favorite white bucket hat and my best shimmery lip gloss. It was the late 1990s after all. My roommates and I walked out of our room and were greeted by the transfer students who lived on our hall. It was their first year at Spelman, but not their first year of college, as they were transferring from other schools. They knew the world better than we did and the body suits they changed into to go back out to Olive Branch showed it. I took my bucket hat and my new me back out to the party and ran into a cute Morehouse student. He smiled at me and I smiled back.

"How you doing?" he said and licked his lips in a fashion that said he'd studied the ways of LL Cool J. "I'm Nick, but my friends call me Freak Nick."

"I'm Amena," I said as we shook hands.

I didn't know how to respond to his nickname. Was this a play on words to allude to Atlanta's infamous Black college spring break event Freaknik? I'd never met a freak in real life. Is that what he meant? New me disappeared and old me stared at him in shock. He responded to assuage my fears.

"See, a ho is somebody who will do anything to anybody. But a freak? Will do everything to somebody," he said and winked at me.

I walked straight back to the dorm and stayed in for the night. There would be no such thing as new me. Church girl me was scared as hell, and scared of hell, which was a wild combination entering my first year in college at an HBCU in a very Black city.

I HAD WANTED TO GO TO SPELMAN SINCE I WAS NINE YEARS OLD. I grew up watching *The Cosby Show*, where the Huxtables were historically Black college graduates and often returned to the famed halls of their fictional alma mater, Hillman College. I became an avid watcher of *Cosby Show* spinoff *A Different World*, which showed young Black people attending Hillman.

In the second season, *A Different World* found its voice and style in director Debbie Allen, and a way better version of the theme song sung by Aretha Franklin. I watched Black girls from all sorts of different places converge on campus to pursue education and to find themselves: Southern belle Whitley Gilbert; Black bohemian and Afrocentric Freddie Brooks; book-smart and ambitious Kimberly Reese; and non-traditional student Jaleesa Vinson.

At this age, I wanted to be a doctor, and my mom's style of parenting included exposing me to anything I decided I wanted to become. My mom was a neonatal nurse. This came with the perks of me looking pretty cool on Career Day when my mom brought Cabbage Patch dolls to my class to explain how she took care of sick babies just after they were born. This also meant my mom knew doctors. She introduced me to a Black woman friend of hers named Dr. Stephanie, a pediatrician and Spelman alumna. Dr. Stephanie walked me into her office and here's where things get fuzzy. My mom didn't go into her office with me, so she doesn't know what Dr. Stephanie said to me. I don't remember what Dr. Stephanie said to me. The only thing my mom and I can both remember is that I walked out of Dr. Stephanie's office and decided I was going to Spelman. Maybe she showed me her degree. Maybe she had some other Spelman insignia around. Whatever she said or showed me, if Spelman indoctrination was her goal, she completed the task.

My elementary school best friend Porsha and I made a pact that we would both attend Spelman even after I moved away in middle school. I spent the rest of junior high and all of high school in San Antonio, but I never forgot about wanting to go to Spelman, my number one college choice.

In middle school, Mom bought me a subscription to *YSB* magazine, which stood for *Young Sisters and Brothers*, and was like a combination of *Essence*, *Ebony*, and *Jet*, but for Black teenagers. Each year *YSB* did a spread about college and highlighted HBCUs you could consider attending. Part of the magazine spread would have rankings and different things I could learn about HBCUs all over the country. Being a teenager of the 1990s, I ripped the pages out of *YSB* and taped them to my wall with my mind set on attending Spelman.

I come from a family where there was a lot of conversation about education. I don't remember in my upbringing having a choice about going to college. I had moved around a lot early on in my life, so the concept of moving someplace where I didn't really know anyone didn't bother me. My mom had settled into Texas life and was a little unsettled that all my college prospects were away from Texas, away from home, away from her. I wanted to apply to Spelman College, Sarah Lawrence College, and Clark Atlanta University.

"Can't you apply to a couple of schools in Texas?" my mom said.

I added Texas A&M and University of Texas at Austin to my list, but I had no intentions of setting foot on either campus. When I applied to college we were just getting used to having a little bit of the internet, but it was still dial-up, noisy modem, and AOL, where you had a limited number of hours you could use the internet. Nothing of the college application process was online, everything was on paper. The only thing I remember doing on the computer was typing out my essays and then printing them.

Applying for college felt like a lot of work: the essays, the application questions, and the letters of recommendation. I started slowing up on the deadlines for my college applications and my mom took notice. She called me into her bathroom and got in my grill. In the 1990s threatening was still an accepted parenting tactic.

"You're going to turn eighteen and you're getting out of this house. You're gonna go someplace. I would like for it to be college for you, but you *are* getting out of this house. Okay?! You're going to sit at that computer and finish your essays and do all the things you're supposed to do."

And because I had some sense, I went ahead and got real productive at that computer.

Back then, college acceptance was an even bigger waiting game. We waited for our acceptance or rejection decisions to arrive via snail mail. If a thin envelope arrived at your home, you knew the first words of the letter were likely to say, "We regret to inform you," but if you received a thick, large envelope, you were almost guaranteed to be reading "Congratulations! You've been accepted."

When my decision letters started pouring in, I was nervous and excited. Sarah Lawrence sent me a thick envelope stating they wanted me to go early decision, but if I did, I would prevent myself from attending Spelman if I got in. I rejected Sarah

Lawrence's offer to go early decision, was accepted into every other school I applied to, but was still waiting for a decision from my application to Spelman.

When I held that thick, large envelope with Spelman's official logo and letterhead on it, I took in a nervous breath and tore through the envelope to get to the papers inside. I'd been accepted! My dorm application was included! My next steps paperwork was ready to be filled out! I WAS GOING TO SPELMAN COLLEGE!

I grew up attending a large, Black, nondenominational, Pentecostal church. Every year, high school graduates received fanfare from the pulpit including announcements of where you were headed after graduation. My church community gave me applause, hugs, and generous pats on the back when I walked across the stage with the other students at church during my graduation year. They sent me to Atlanta with a love offering large enough to start my first bank account and cover the cost of my books.

In my first few weeks of college, I ran into my childhood friend Porsha when I was in line getting my student ID. We kept our pact to each other!

I discovered the astonishing number of words that could be added to "shawty" to make a phrase each time I walked from campus through the West End: shawty long legs, chocolate shawty, shawty lip gloss, shawty red bone, tall shawty.

I gave up on new me and decided to be old me in a new place. I joined a campus ministry after meeting a sophomore student named Kia whose hair was so laid I had to find out her name and where she got her hair done. She told me she got her hair done in Marietta, a suburb of Atlanta that might as well have been Timbuktu to carless me. She told me she was a part of a campus ministry at Spelman called New Generation and that I should come to morning prayer, which was held Monday through Friday on the steps of Sisters Chapel at seven a.m. I decided this was the way. Once a church girl, always a church girl, and with all the fine men across the street at Morehouse and at Clark, it seemed a cadre of other Christian girls could be a place to help me stay focused on my books and make my family and church community proud.

I went to morning prayer, and there were other church girl first-year students like me, and there were upperclasswomen who were sophomores, juniors, and seniors. Two of the seniors confessed to us they had made the decision not to date for the entire four years of their college careers, and they were so glad they did now that they were about to graduate.

I looked at both of them. Flawless skin, nice clothes. I didn't say anything, but inside I thought, *But you're pretty, why would you not date with all these beautiful men around here?! *points at Morehouse College across the street**

Everyone introduced themselves, where they were from, and what year they were in school. We prayed for each other to stand strong and survive temptation. We prayed for our campus to come to Jesus the Christ because what else were we sent to school for except to evangelize the whole place?! Spelman's then–school motto was "Our Whole School for Christ," and we took that shit to heart!

A Different World had shown me the diversity of young Black women, but Spelman showed me there was a whole world of us. Spelman had Black girls from up north with their New York accents and Timberlands and door knockers. There were Black girls from the Midwest, from Chicago and Detroit, with their unique hairstyles. There were West Coast Black girls with their breezy attitudes and eclectic fashion. There were Texas girls, mostly from Dallas and Houston, with personalities as big as the state they were from. There were girls from down South with a sweet twang to their accents. There were Black girls from the Caribbean and Black girls from many countries in Africa. There were headwraps and braids and straight hair down to the hips.

There were Black girls who were Protestant church girls like me, who grew up Baptist, Pentecostal, Lutheran, AME. There were Black girls who grew up Catholic. I didn't know even Black people were Catholic until I went to Spelman. Sunday mornings I'd watch the Black girls who were Catholic head to mass en masse. There were Black girls who were Muslim, who wore hijab, some orthodox and some Nation of Islam. There were Black girls who grew up Bahá'í, Buddhist, and atheist.

Black girls who were shy and modest and Black girls who had no problem letting their hips and tiddies swing. Black girls who were straight and Black girls who were queer. All shapes, all sizes, different languages and slang, various shades of us participating in the tradition of so many Black women before us in getting an education.

Spelman was like the New York City of Black girls. Every different type of Black girl I could imagine was represented on campus, in my dorm and in my classes. I didn't fully realize what breathing in the air of this was showing me until many years after I graduated.

In my high school, it felt like you had to choose what kind of Black girl you were going to be. A church girl. A nerdy girl. A Black girl who was down with all the latest Black girl fashions. Even if you were multiple things at the same time, it felt like there wasn't room for you to be. If you were a nerdy Black girl, you couldn't be fashionable or pretty. If you were a church girl, sometimes you had to choose between your church identity and school popularity.

When I arrived at Spelman, I wasn't the only one or the first one or the cool one or the nerdy one. Being in a Black girl and Black woman–centric environment afforded us the freedom to learn to be ourselves, to learn to embrace the many facets of us.

I started to feel like I hadn't just randomly picked Spelman, but instead had been drawn, maybe even called to Spelman. Who else was going to pray for the girls about to take the club bus to Club Kaya and Esso's?! The spring of my first year in college, Freaknik (the event, not Freak Nick the person) was a buzz around campus. Many of us had only seen images of Freaknik on TV or heard about it from friends or older siblings or cousins. The local news was showing that many people in the city were getting tired of Freaknik, deciding to leave town until the rush of visitors passed or choosing to stay home to not be caught in the intentional traffic jams replete with handheld camcorders and ass shaking.

My new campus ministry Spelman sisters and I felt no such pull to this event. We took our mission with the same fervor of the Bible prophet Nehemiah. We needed to "stand in the gap" and "stand on the wall" for our Spelman sisters, for the AUC community, *for the world*. As many first-year students decided to venture out into the Freaknik streets, my ministry sisters and I met on the steps of Sisters Chapel to pray against the spirit of Freaknik, against the lure of lust, to pray for Jesus the Christ to *save our city*. That year was the last year of Freaknik as anybody knew it and we took prayer credit for it. Obviously Freaknik had disbanded because of our fervent prayers. We had prayed the Freaknik away. I hadn't seen Freak Nick either. Maybe we had prayed him away too!

The truth is, Freaknik was on its last legs anyway. Police presence, the disdain of city leadership, rowdy out-of-towners, and girls and women finding the Freaknik streets to be filled with disregard and disrespect had caused Freaknik to fizzle over the years from a wholesome Black college spring break, to a festival of music and young antics, to an event that had more memories of days gone by than current relevance. We didn't know this at the time. For all we knew our righteous prayers had *availed* much.

A couple of years ago, Hulu released a Freaknik documentary. Whispers and check-ins burned through the AUC alumni network. What years would be featured? Whose parents or grandparents would be found twerking or doing the butterfly on national TV? I texted a few of my ministry sisters, now a mix of in church and out of church, and said, "You know who doesn't have to worry about being in this documentary? We don't! Because no camcorders caught us praying on campus."

I graduated from Spelman having spent my first three years in campus ministry and my last year in local church ministry. After graduation, I spent nearly a decade performing poetry and speaking in churches and Christian settings before expanding my career and my spirituality beyond those spaces. Every couple of years I returned to Spelman for homecoming or for my college reunion. I got to know some of the students I'd been in class with (but not in ministry with) and heard tell of their college exploits: the club bus, the boyfriends, the girlfriends, the house parties. All things I didn't experience in school, but now we were meeting as alumnae, as young professionals, as rising stars in our respective fields, as single people, divorcées and married folks, as parents and as childfree and childless.

This time I took more time to get to know my sisters and siblings, rather than assuming I knew their lives and how to pray for them. For once, I didn't have to be old me or new me. I could just be myself exactly as I was at that moment, rubbing shoulders with the women who had learned about womanism, freedom, and liberation in the same classes as I did.

Between being a Spelman grad, having grown up in a Black

church, and having been raised by and around confident Black women, I gained the tenacity to enter a lot of spaces where some people thought I didn't belong. It was instilled in me from going to Spelman there was not a place as a Black woman that I didn't deserve to be in. I deserved to be at the table just like anybody else. I deserved to build a table just like anybody else.

My Spelman sisters and siblings showed me I could be a church girl. I could love hip hop. I could be a nerd. I could be Southern. I could be shy. I could let my hair, the way I dressed, my makeup, my style, my belief system, how I lived my life, evolve as I did. I could Black Girl however I wanted to, and that is a lesson that will stick with me forever.

A RESPONSE TO THE QUESTION: WHEN ARE YOU GOING TO HAVE KIDS

My husband and I don't have kids. There is nothing super remarkable about this. We are just two people who love each other living our lives without children. In a bar, in a restaurant, at a dinner party, this doesn't matter to most people. We find other things to talk about, like TV shows we love, how much we love our dogs, or memes that made us laugh. But if there's one place where being married a certain amount of time with no children will not stand, it's in church. If there's one place where people feel a special license to get in your business, it's in church.

In church, small talk goes one of two ways, especially if you're a woman. Option one is questions about your relationship status: "Are you married?" "Are you dating?" "Why are you still single?" Option two is about your parenting possibilities:

"Do you have kids?" "Why don't you have kids?" "When are you going to have kids?" "When are you going to have more kids?"

Sometimes people ask us about having kids because I'm a Black woman and my husband's a white man with red hair and they wanna know how all this DNA is gonna shake out. Sometimes they ask because they think a woman has no purpose if she doesn't have a spouse and kids. Sometimes they ask because they have kids and don't know what else to talk about if you don't have kids. Sometimes they ask because they are bad at small talk, and sometimes, they ask because they are too damn nosy for their own good.

But they ask anyway, as if it's their business, as if I owe them an explanation as to what my uterus is or isn't doing. Most times I nod my way out of it, deflect my way out of it, polite my way to the next topic of conversation, which means I endure a lot of disrespectful shit like . . .

Just adopt . . .
Just do fertility treatment . . .
Geritol got me pregnant . . .
Do it this way . . .
Do it that way . . .
Get drunk . . .
Don't drink . . .
Use essential oils and rub them counterclockwise . . .

. . . And all manner of unsolicited terrible advice.

But this particular day—I'd had it. After telling myself I wouldn't take any more church gigs, I took one, for Easter. My husband traveled with me, and I was supposed to perform a poem to be captured on video for a church's Easter service. It had been a while since I'd worked in a church environment, so I had nearly forgotten how the small talk goes.

We were greeted by a woman the church assigned to host us and make sure we had plenty of water, tea, and snacks as needed. She started the small talk with Option One to confirm that we were indeed married, even asking how many years we'd been married. This is its own subtle kid check. If you're a newlywed, it's cute that you don't have kids. Three to five years married? Understandable depending on your age. Seven plus years married? It is the job of every church person you meet to become an impromptu reproductive endocrinologist. You must have a problem and they must have a solution. Maybe you're not doing it. Maybe you're not doing it right. Either way it's now their self-appointed job to fix it, or it's your job to convince them you're doing everything you can to fix it. It only takes this woman a couple of minutes to reach Option Two.

"Do you have any kids?" she said.

"Nope," we said.

"Are you trying?" she said.

Yes. Mm-hmm you read that right. A grown woman whom we just met asked us if we were trying to have kids. A grown woman whom we just met was attempting to inquire about our sex life or our medical history or our personal health and family decisions.

I wished I would have cussed her clean out. She deserved to get cussed clean out. But I couldn't cuss her out. Not because I didn't want to. Not because I was being too nice. But because I can never think of the right cuss words in the moment. I am a woman who broods and stews, a slow thinker. I have never improvised very well. But give me forty-eight hours to seventeen months and I will have every cuss word ready for a moment that is already well in the past.

Someone interrupted us. I never got the chance to answer her back. I wished I had a prepared response for times like this, something I could say that could quickly shut these conversations down. On the way home, it hit me. I thought of the perfect thing to say. I rehearsed it in my head as if I could redo the entire conversation.

"Do you have any kids?" she'd say.

"Nope," I'd say.

"Are you trying?" she'd say.

"Are you in a relationship?" I'd say.

"Yes, my husband and I have been married for several years," she'd say.

And I'd say, "Do you suck dick?"

She'd gasp. Clutch her pearls. Look at me as if I have said the most offensive thing.

I'd say, "Oh is that too personal? Too private? Is that none of my business? Is that something you wanted to remain between you and your spouse?"

Then I'd get quiet, hope it starts to sink in. Maybe she'll think about how it feels to have someone ask you a very personal question in a very public moment. Maybe she'll consider the layers of personal reasons that are a factor into why people do or don't have kids. Maybe in the future she'll decide favorite TV shows, recent good books, or best and worst movies are the types of questions that make for better small talk.

Maybe she won't think any of this. Maybe she'll be too busy scoffing at why people who seem happily married can't get it together and just have some kids already. She would probably clutch her pearls that I had the audacity to say the word *dick* and then to say *suck* in front of it. Her silence would tell me maybe she wasn't sucking dick, which would leave me the room to ask her the most important question of all.

"Are *you* trying?"

ON FINDING A THERAPIST

went to therapy for the first time when I was twenty-five years old. I had been recently hired for my first job in corporate America, where for the first time I was getting paid to be a writer. Around this time, I had also left a church for the first time, the same church I had been attending since college.

Church was not just the place where I was practicing my religion or being encouraged in my faith, it was also the center of my social life. Leaving this church meant walking away from my social life as I knew it. I went from going to church four times a week to sitting at a table full of margaritas with my new coworkers and friends. In my new life, I was trying to go on dates. Sometimes they were going well, most times they weren't. I was very uncomfortable, even with the thought of sitting across the table at coffee or at dinner with a man I found attractive.

At my new job, there were three other women who were hired in my same position: one Black woman, one Korean woman, and one white woman. We were the corporate version of The Cheetah Girls or the Pussycat Dolls. Maybe we could have been the Paper Dolls, but that sounds like more of a Dunder Mifflin thing. None of us were married, but all of us were at different stages between being in a very committed dating relationship or still casually dating.

The other Black woman, let's call her Aisha, and I had cubicles right next to each other. I had met a guy, and we were just getting to know each other. Talking to him made me very nervous. I went in her cubicle a lot to talk to her about him. Processing. Processing. Processing. Overprocessing. I couldn't figure out what to do about this, what to do about that, and this was not the first dating situation she had listened to me attempting to process.

One afternoon she looked at me and she said, "You know what? I don't really think I can help you figure this out. I think what you need is a therapist."

The side of my face felt numb. My arms frozen at my sides. I couldn't tell what it was I'd said to her that made her feel like I needed to go to therapy. I was somewhere between feeling embarrassed and insulted, and really grateful and helped.

I talked to her a little bit longer and then I went right to my cubicle and started googling therapist options. After a couple of pre-consultation calls, I settled on a therapist, an older white woman with a soothing voice. Before my first appointment, she asked me to write a letter and describe the areas of my life where I hoped to grow during therapy.

I wrote about the church, about God, about my parents' divorce, about things I was processing from my family of origin. I decided to pen a letter like I was writing home with stories of my platoon. I wrote and wrote and wrote. Anyway, it was the Before Times. I put a wax seal on the envelope and sent it back to my therapist via pigeon.

On the TV show *Insecure*, when Issa is trying to convince Molly she needs to go to therapy, Molly doesn't take it very well at first. The idea you would have a friend that would look at you and say, "I think you need to go to therapy," could make you feel defensive. Could make you wonder, *Why would you say that about me? What's wrong with me?* It can be the most loving thing to suggest therapy to someone, and it can be the most loving thing you can do for yourself to submit to the process of therapy. But it can also be hard.

I saw my first therapist for over a year. Then I took a therapy break, until stress and life transition compelled me to seek out a therapist again. Since then, I have had some really hilarious and out-of-hand therapy experiences. I signed up for online therapy, one of those services where you never see your therapist in person but you could online chat as well as schedule video or phone calls. My first assigned therapist was really helpful. She was the first person to name I had a lot of unprocessed grief. But the downside to her was whenever we had our sessions, she was always busy doing a little bit of something else. During one of our sessions, someone rang the doorbell to give her a package.

"Who is that at the door? Who is that? I was not expecting anybody," she said while I was talking through my grief and trauma.

I told myself, *She works from home. She can't control if the package got delivered.* The next session while I'm telling all my business I hear someone humming in the background. I keep talking, but after a while I get quiet because I don't know what's going on.

She finally says, "I'm sorry. I'm babysitting my grandson, and he normally doesn't keep this type of noise."

This lady seemed very sweet, but I realized she could not be my therapist. You cannot babysit your grandson while I'm trying to process my griefs and traumas in a therapy session with you.

I signed up in the online account to be assigned to a new therapist. When I went to talk through my grief with her, she said, "No, honey, we don't want to claim that! We speak life!" I even did a pre-consultation with a potential new therapist and her smoke detector was chirping so loud in her office I couldn't remember what I wanted to say to her.

After a couple of false starts and terrible tries, I eventually found a therapist I liked. In the past few years I've had two Black women therapists who held space for me, helped me process grief, pain, and anxiety, understood when I needed to attend a session wearing a bonnet or a shower cap because I was in the middle of wash day, pursed their lips together and said mm-hmm when white America realized for the umpteenth time America was racist . . . *again*.

In session we've talked about *The Color Purple*, *Waiting to Exhale*, *Parable of the Sower*, the ancestors, the Black church, and why consent is required for sexual moments and for our hair.

Sometimes my therapy experience has been a comedy of errors, but finding the right therapist where I could be myself and bring my full self to session was worth it. Therapy is for those people who have those problems, and therapy is for you and your problems too. It is a healing space to bring your questions, insecurities, feelings, and experiences as you begin what will likely be a lifelong healing journey. Like any relationship, finding the right therapist takes time and patience. I am so thankful my coworker had the courage to encourage me to go to therapy, because it changed my life for the better.

Even if I have to offer new batteries as a solution to that chirping smoke detector.

LETTER TO MY BLACK WOMAN THERAPIST

Dear My Black Woman Therapist,

Since our last session, I have listened to Beyoncé's *Lemonade*, Solange's *A Seat at the Table*, and ALL of India.Arie's albums. I have meditated and I am on the way to perfecting warrior one. I have also nearly cussed out a family member. But I didn't cuss them out. And you know what you taught me that is? Growth. *Natasha Rothwell's Kelli hand gesture from Insecure*

I just wanted to say thank you for the detour through *Women of Brewster Place* we took last week. How as soon as I brought up that brick wall at the end where Oprah Winfrey and Jackée Harry and Lynn Whitfield tore that wall down with their bare hands, you nodded and pointed at the air with your pen. How I told you that's what my healing journey felt like at the moment.

Thank you for understanding every single reference to *The Color Purple*, including but not limited to: Celie Finna Shave Mista, I Said Fine with Me, Girl Child Ain't Safe in a House Full of Mens, Did I Ever Ask You for Anything, Sofia Home Now, and Harpo Who Dis Woman. For pointing your three fingers across the screen, same as I did, and saying, "Til you do right by me!" with no need to even finish the rest of the sentence. Knowing how much I needed a family member, the world, and myself to do right by me too.

There's a place in the Bible where it talks about God keeping track of our tears and sorrows, recording each one in a book. And I know you're reading this like, is she quoting from the Bible?! Because you know I haven't read my Bible in a minute. But I also wanted to say thank you for being a spiritual reflection of this, for helping me keep record of the tears and sorrows I carry with me. Thanks for receiving my anger and cuss words: about the job, my work, relationships, family, about the difficulty of finding the proper hair products, about the heartbreak of a silk press meeting the rain or too much humidity, about grief, about the finality of death and the absurdity of life. Thank you for the reminder my grief and my rage aren't things to be put to the side like someone's unfortunate dislike of Beyoncé. Wait. Actually, in our next session, can we talk about how this is not a thing that can be put to the side?! Like did they even listen to "Formation"?!

Thank you for your patience when I desperately needed to put on lip balm or lotion in the middle of a session because you understood it is a cardinal sin of being Black to have chapped lips or ashy skin. Thank you for every *mm-hmm* and *gurl* and *okay?!* and *I know that's right.* For reminding me every shut eye ain't sleep and every goodbye ain't gone. For reminding me to light a candle. For encouraging me to pray to whomever I need to and reminding me I have the permission not to pray at all if that is best for my well-being.

Thanks for seeing my bonnet and nodding your head when I pointed to it and said *wash day* or *braids appointment* or *I just took my braids down*. Thanks for telling me I don't have to pull it together to come to our sessions. That if I can barely make it out of the bed, we can video chat from there.

Thanks for reminding me where home is, in my own skin. For honoring the spiritual traditions I grew up with and the new spiritual practices I'm still developing. Thanks for the copies of books by Black authors you keep on your bookshelf. For understanding why I was more tired than usual after the halftime show featuring Kendrick or Beyoncé or Usher or anybody Black for that matter.

Thank you for every moment where you said the equivalent of, "Go ahead and free yourself," just like Fantasia would want us to do. Thank you for all the moments you let our session get quiet, to let me hear the words I'd just said, to remind me, I can be free too.

When it starts to settle in with me, there's a certain knowing smile you get. You'll remind me of how I used to not be able to handle that conversation or navigate that relationship or talk about certain things without feeling like my whole body was shaking in a way I couldn't control. You'll offer me something like that healing high five/hand hold that Oprah gave to each of her guests on Super Soul Sunday. You'll remind me I may have plenty of healing and growth left to do but I've also come a mighty long way. *Church quickening*

I know it's against the rules for us to be friends. I know we only have a limited amount of kikis we can share. I know if I ran into you in the grocery store or if you ran into me at the beauty supply store we would both respectfully nod and act as if we don't know each other. I know our sessions are mostly about me: my healing, my growth, my pet peeves, my childhood, and all the shit I'm still unlearning, the coworker who tried it, the coworker who tried it again during Black History Month no less. But I want you to know, I started being able to get out of bed because of the work we're doing here. I found some joy again. I learned how to be gentle with myself, how to receive help, how to allow myself to give and receive love.

I wish all your clients were as enjoyable and hilarious as I am. I know they're not but that's okay. That's why I'm here. I wanted you to know your work is important. I wanted you to know how much it matters to me to look across the room or screen and see your skin, your nose, your cheekbones, your hair, a reflection of me, of the women who raised me, of the Black women who are in community with me. I imagine your job isn't easy. I hope for you to have many spaces in your life like the one you offer me. A place to show up exactly as you are. I hope you get to relish your own aha moments and the moments your clients finally hear the thing you've been trying to get them to see. But most of all, I wish for you the peace, gentleness, and care you have poured into me.

See you next session,

Amena

WAITING TO EXHALE, SHOOP SHOOP, AND WHY DOES BRANDY'S VOICE DO THIS TO ME?!

*Takes *Waiting to Exhale* soundtrack out of the CD case. Slides CD into the CD player. Sings "Shoop shoop shoop shoop bae doop" exactly like Whitney Houston.* Just kidding. I don't have a CD player anymore.

I stumbled upon my first Terry McMillan books when I was too young to be reading them. But it was the 1990s and our parents gave us plenty of time unsupervised. Like many elder millennials and young Gen Xers, I discovered these books because an adult Black woman in my life was reading them. In my case, it was my mom.

There are Black women of a certain age that loved and felt so seen by Terry McMillan's books. There was a time in the 1990s where you could go to nearly any Black woman's house and see the following on her coffee table: a copy of *Essence* magazine, *Ebony* magazine, *Jet* magazine, and one or two copies of sundry books by Terry McMillan. A lot of the earlier books I'd read that were written by Black authors were set in the past. They weren't written in what would've been considered contemporary or modern times. My gateway into Terry McMillan's books was her novel *Waiting to Exhale*, a story centered on the lives and relationships of four Black women friends in their twenties and thirties. The perspectives of these grown Black women intrigued me, especially as a teenager. Also, my first sex scenes I ever read were written by Terry McMillan. I remember thinking, *Ooh, this is nasty, but I'm going to keep reading it!*

Terry McMillan's books were so popular many of them were turned into movies, including *How Stella Got Her Groove Back*, *Disappearing Acts*, *A Day Late and a Dollar Short*, and *Waiting to Exhale*. When I was growing up, my mom always had a small number of women friends she really loved and was close to. Whenever they would come over, they would spend the first part of the night letting me hang out with them, but at a certain time, my mom would put me to bed so they could have grown woman talk.

My favorite movie of all time is *The Godfather*. We don't need to talk about *Godfather III* or that director's cut I can never remember the name of. At the end of the first *Godfather* movie there is a scene where Kay asks Michael if he is doing the criminal acts it seems like he's doing. I am yelling at the screen, "Of course he is, Kay! You married a gangsta! You married into a gangsta family! When you went to Connie's wedding, your then-boyfriend, now husband, told you a cheeky yet scary story about his father threatening a man to put either his signature or his brains on a contract! Michael did everything they said he did, Kay!"

But of course, Michael lies to her, and she believes him.

Right before the credits roll you see her staring into his office while the other capos and made men arrive to kiss the ring (I mean, isn't this literally how "kiss the ring" the cliché arrived in pop culture!), and we watch Michael slowly close the door in Kay's face.

When I was growing up, I was Kay, except my mom wasn't a gangsta and she wasn't lying to me. I wanted her to believe I could be just as fun to hang out with as her girlfriends were. I could be grown. Sophisticated. It didn't matter that I was too young to know how to spell *sophisticated*. Both Kay and I had the door slowly closed in our face. My mom and her friends would gently close the door to my room in my face and go downstairs, where they would talk their grown woman talk. I was resolute that one day I'd have some women friends to stay up late and chat with too. My mom's friendships showed me the friendships in *Waiting to Exhale* were possible in real life.

There were a lot of ways Terry McMillan's work influenced my mom's generation of Black women, what they found to be true about their dating lives and how they navigated choosing paths different from their own mothers', aunts', and grand-mothers'. They felt free to get divorced if their marriages weren't working. They felt free to enjoy sex and not be shy about it. They felt free to admit when they didn't know what to do with their lives.

THEN IN 1995, THE MOVIE *WAITING TO EXHALE* WAS RELEASED, STAR-ring Whitney Houston, Loretta Devine, Lela Rochon, and An-gela Bassett, a quadrumvirate of Black womanhood. These four women. Yes. Damn and yes.

Whitney Houston was a gorgeous human being. The early scenes of the film are locked in on Whitney Houston's eyes, nose, mouth, and the sound of her speaking voice. Her character doesn't sing in the movie ever, but even the lilt to Whitney Houston's speaking voice was musical. We have Whitney Houston's character Savannah, who is moving to a new city and is trying to figure out how to move on from her married ex.

Lela Rochon is playing Robin in this film, and Lela Rochon is that girl, okay?! The way she was dressed in this movie, the hair choices, the number of Black films Lela Rochon was in at this time. *That girl.* If *Waiting to Exhale*'s cast was like the Golden Girls, Robin is the Betty White of the clique, she is the Rose. She is not the sharpest person among them. She sometimes misses the context clues of what is going on in her life. She is also single, and she and Savannah both have men in their lives that are no good for them.

Angela Bassett's character Bernadine is married when we begin this movie and we watch her experience a great life adjustment. Her husband announces to her the marriage is over as he has decided to be in a relationship with someone else.

And then we have Loretta Devine playing Gloria, a single mom with a son who is approaching his last year of high school. Her ex-husband, David, is trying to be in her son's life and also is a sort of remedy for times when she feels lonely or needs sexual healing. Her ex-husband has come out as gay and here is where this film and the book are an unfortunate time capsule.

In a retooling of these characters, David's gayness would not have been an indictment of why Gloria or other cis-het Black women would remain single. David could have come out to his wife. She and David both would have had to process his sexual identity and what that would mean for their relationship with each other and how they would co-parent their son.

Their son, Tarik, could have had space to process his own feelings about his dad's sexual identity. A family therapy session could have been had. Their son could learn to eschew toxic masculinity, that his "manhood" as a cis-het young man was not ruined or tainted by the fact that his father is not the toxically masculine cis-het man he thought he was.

In therapy David would have space to see the beauty in his gayness, Gloria would have space to rediscover her wants and needs beyond her roles as mother and wife, and Tarik would have discussed what he's learning about the expansiveness of gender fluidity and sexual identity. Then Gloria, Tarik, and David could have had a Lena Waithe–produced sitcom spin-off called *Willing to Learn* instead of *Waiting to Inhale* or *Rushing to Exhale* or *Wondering When to Breathe*. If only the 1990s had been more evolved.

Back to *Waiting to Exhale*, the movie. We are meeting each of them on New Year's Eve and we follow them for a year of their lives because the film also closes at where their lives are at the following New Year's Eve. My favorite scene involves Gloria and Marvin. Marvin is played by Gregory Hines, and I need to speak about this for a moment. Gregory Hines is not an actor until *Waiting to Exhale* I would have ever viewed as someone who is sexy or is a sex symbol. The main thing I had in my mind about Gregory Hines was that he was a tap dancer. But here we have Gregory Hines moving in as an across-the-street neighbor to Gloria.

We find him in a muscle shirt moving his things. Gloria does not even peep game that he is the neighbor based on how he's dressed. Because the story is set in Phoenix, Arizona, her assumption is, he is helping her new neighbors move into the neighborhood, her new neighbors she assumes are likely not Black. Gloria sashays her beautiful curvy self across the street, sits down, and does a little tea outreach. She's trying to find out from this man *Wherefore, pray tell, who is the family moving into this house.*

Of course, it becomes this funny exchange because he is the family. He is the neighbor! When she discovers this, she does what any good Southern woman would do. We're not given where all these characters are from before they arrived in Phoenix. But based on Loretta Devine's accent, it always gives something Southern, and she is showing me some very Southern things in her way of being. She has a moment where she offers food to Marvin, knowing he probably doesn't have his kitchen unpacked.

It is my dream as a Southern woman myself, who comes from at least four generations of Southern women, to always have food made if someone were to need food or come by and need something to eat or if I ended up with a last-minute houseguest. There was something inspiring in Loretta Devine's Gloria, about the preparedness of a Southern woman who feels the need to potentially have enough of a little something to eat to share with anyone who needs it.

Gloria tells Marvin, "It's just leftovers. Collard greens and corn bread, some candied yams, a little potato salad, fried chicken, peach cobbler, and a few slices of ham." Gloria becomes a flirty version of Shirley Caeser's "You Name It." She sashays herself back across the street and says out loud to herself, "Is he watching me?" And of course he was watching!

My second favorite scene is when Angela Bassett's character Bernadine burns all her soon-to-be ex-husband's shit. When we first meet Bernadine, she's dressed beautifully, makeup done, jewelry sparkling, dressed for her husband's usual black-tie New Year's Eve work event. Her husband says, "I think we should have a change of plan tonight," and then has the audacity to announce to her he's been having an affair with his new secretary (*belts out* *Was your lover and your seck-uh-tary!*) and he wants to take his new, young hhwhhite secretary to his work event and flaunt her all around the place. This man, that she had been married to all these years, helped build his company and his career. This man just all of a sudden decided this shit is inconvenient now?! He just doesn't want to be with her anymore after she had the two kids and everything?!

She takes in this news, sitting at her Clair Huxtable-esque vanity. There is a lot required in a vanity: a brush that matches a comb, that matches some kind of big powder puff thing you put on your face. This is the vanity little girl Amena really thought she was going to have when she became a grown woman. Those of you that watched *The Cosby Show* growing up, remember how Clair would sit at that vanity and brush her hair every night. I thought to myself, *This is some grown woman shit, I'm going to do this too.* To be clear, I'm grown and I do not have a vanity. Also, I do not have the kind of hair that can be brushed the way Clair Huxtable and Bernadine were brushing their hair.

We watch Bernadine descend into a very deep level of sadness. The next time we see her she is dressed in a raggedy bathrobe, sends her kids off to school, and decides she needs to burn her husband's shit down to the ground.

You know how they have these smash rooms where you can go and bang TVs and break glass and stuff?! They should also have some type of a *Waiting to Exhale* Bernadine-themed rage room. You could take clothes off the rack, stuff them through the sunroof of the faux car, light a cigarette, and burn everything: dress shoes, sneakers, suits, and the car. If I had another me, I would start a franchise of rage rooms for the angry Black woman, because we have a lot of valid reasons to be angry!

THE *WAITING TO EXHALE* SOUNDTRACK HAD SOME BANGERS. WE have Whitney Houston's "Exhale (Shoop Shoop)." We also have Toni Braxton's "Let It Flow." We have Brandy's "Sittin' Up in My Room," and we have a quintessential tune from this movie: Mary J. Blige's "Not Gon' Cry."

This is one of those songs I remember listening to on my little clock radio in my room. That sounded old as hell. Anyways, I remember singing my guts out, even though I hadn't lived through any of these things that Bernadine went through and Mary J. Blige sang about.

The other song on this soundtrack that needs to be discussed is "Count on Me," featuring Brandy, CeCe Winans, and Whitney Houston. The vocals are unmatched and unparalleled. I love a good friendship song and there is just something about "Count on Me" that touches my heart every time.

sings loudly "Please believe me when I say, *count on count on count on count on meeeeeeee!* Oh yes you can. I know I can. Sho can."

Waiting to Exhale is a time capsule of Black culture, Black history, Black herstory. What were Black women concerned about? What were Black women wanting out of their lives? What were the beliefs and statements that were problematic? Where have we learned to do better? What are the themes in this story that are still present in Black women's lives today?

Following in the tradition of my mom and her friends, of Gloria, Bernadine, Savannah, and Robin, I gather with my friends in the corner of a coffee shop, in the nook of a restaurant, leaning back on the couch in my living room or theirs with our shoes off. I have garnered a beautiful community of women to walk through life with: writers, artists, activists, some established in their corporate careers, some starting their second or third businesses, some single, some married, some divorced, some parents of dogs and/or children.

Sometimes we treat ourselves to lavish dinners, other times we gather things from our own refrigerators and cabinets and make a kind of bootleg potluck. Some days we plan to gather for brunch and then decide we'd rather gather for early breakfast because we don't want to wait in line or listen to a deejay or see an Insta-worthy grass wall while we catch up on each other's lives. We celebrate each other's birthdays, promotions, anniversaries, weddings, and divorces. We hold each other's grief and broken hearts. We cuss and pray, sometimes at the same time. We cook food for each other. We check in. We love each other for as long as life allows.

What I learned from *Waiting to Exhale* more than anything is how important the friendships of Black women are. How important it is for us to gather and sit in front of each other's coffee tables. How maybe sometimes life should be less "That's a good man, Savannah" and more "That's a good friend, Savannah." And most importantly, Black women always need healthy amounts of shoop shoop bae doop.

GIRLFRIENDS POEM

We find our friendships in coffee shops and at lunch
  tables
In greenrooms and quiet corners of other people's
  parties
We skip the shallow small talk and pleasantries
We turn public places into living rooms

We bare our souls
We decide not to hide where the extra folds
Have made their home on our bodies
We drink wine, margaritas, and chai
Tell jokes over guacamole, queso, and tortilla chips
Toast to cupcakes and butter rolls
Because who needs champagne when we can dish over
  donuts

Calorie counting don't count here
Your round hips are welcome here
Here we celebrate cellulite
And stomachs that never returned to taut after gaining
    weight or birthing children

Here
We no longer need to impress people who care nothing
    about us
Here
We preach acceptance to each other
We say to each other
Girl
Love yourself
The way you love me
The way you forgive me when I'm late
Even though I say every time I'm gon' be on time
The way you let me cry when I'm angry
The way you let me vent when I want to be mean to the
    world and to myself
When you watch me carry my stress into panic attacks
    and migraines
The way you pray for my soul to find rest

We walk together
Sweat together
Lift the weight of this world
Until our arms and souls are stronger for it
We mend each other by saying things like,
"Remember that time when . . ."
Like when I was head over heels in love with
    that man

Who looked so good but could never manage to tell the
    truth
And that job you hated
How I called you to make you laugh
And you pretended I was a customer
For the coworker who always eavesdropped on our
    conversations
Or when I was so broke we switched cars to play tricks on
    the repo man

Sometimes when we meet, we tell each other hard truths
About the parents and babies we've lost
About grieving
About jobs and promotions that mean new locations and
    cities
About starting over
About finding new ways to do the same old things
About first dates that never make it to second ones

We decide not to judge
You never know the pain another woman hides
Behind insecurity, too much mascara, or an ill-fitting outfit
Until you have not only walked in her shoes
But also know her pain and wounds
How she survived her scars
That it is brave to look yourself in the eyes every day
And decide to love the woman who stares back

We are more than bestie or BFF
We are tribe and sisterhood
We are not what reality TV tries to convince us woman
    friendship is

We do not throw martini glasses or spiteful words
We hold each other up
With grace and laughs and love
Just because

Girl
We are here
Until we stop hiding our grays
Until the generation after us begins to take care of us
Until we help them stand while they help us sit
Until we turn our porches into town hall meetings
Drink wine to stave off sickness

And can barely hear out of either ear for dancing too close
    to the speakers
At all the parties and concerts
With no regrets

With no, "We haven't dreamed and done that yet"

We take the word *friend*
And carry its meaning in the wrinkles of our hands
We take each other's secrets and stories
To the grave with us

PART 5

THE AWKWARDNESS OF FINDING COUPLE FRIENDS, WHY EVERY COUPLE NEEDS TWO BATHROOMS, AND OTHER THINGS I'VE LEARNED ABOUT RELATIONSHIPS

LUNGS

I've had my lungs a long time
Taken in many breaths absentmindedly
With no thought of where they come from
Or if they will soon end
But your chest, your skin
Has taught me to count and enjoy
Revel and bask in these inhales and exhales
Enjoy how our lungs cleave to each other
Waves of breath as if we are our own sea and beach
You look at me and cause sunrises in my insides
All warm and orange and purple and new

We listen to crickets sing
Cricket choirs in leaf robes
Alto soprano tenor

Into the night
Watch stars and leaves ballet and plié
Enjoy each other's conversation as if it were delicacy

When our sentences have ceased
We are left there, holding hands and breathing
We are breathing
Because we can
Because we should
Take full advantage of these inhales and exhales
Because every time we feel breath in our nostrils
Is an opportunity to say thank you we're here
Thank you we survived
Thank you to God for making us in the first place

Me and you
We run through hip hop shows
Still rocking our b-boy b-girl clothes
We don't let being grown change us
You rock your turntables and I jump in and lip-sync a few
    verses

We make home where our hearts live
We make love with fingertips and rhymes
Taking romantic lines out of the things
Method Man and LL Cool J say

This morning we woke up before the alarm went off
You lying on your back
Me scooting over inch by inch until I laid my face on the
    left side of your chest

One hand in the middle of your torso
Talking about the goofy dreams we had last night

I made you laugh
Felt your belly shake underneath me
Realized I can't imagine life without you now
Don't even want to imagine elderly me reminiscing about
    you
Telling the stories that characterize the life we lived
    together
Keeping a few stories to myself
Because those stories were ours
And no one but you would understand them anyway

I understand now the way Sade sings
The way a love like this changes you
I tell you I love you
Any and every time I can
Because I want you to have a bank account full of I love
    yous
High yielding, interest bearing, with no penalty
More I love yous to live off of when we get older
And can barely move our hips and lips
I want my I love yous to play inside your head
Like old records on repeat
I want my I love yous to stick with you
Like oatmeal on a cold morning
Like my cousin's ribs on the smoker in the summer

Tonight, after we chat about the day
We'll say good night

And when I wake up in the middle of the night
I'll put my hand on your chest
Feel it rise with each breath
Kiss you, whisper I love you in your sleep
And be grateful

BED TIME

When my husband and I met, both of our lives were in shambles. He lived with his parents, recovering from a devastating divorce, and I was renting a room from a friend of a friend while recovering from my failed attempt at an artist career. When we got married, we had very few possessions between us. He had a hand-me-down couch, leather chair, and ottoman, a budget mattress, turntables, and saxophones. I had an old bubble TV, a thin, unleavened mattress, a hand-me-down bed frame, an excessive amount of books and journals, and a dinette set. His possessions were taking up space in his parents' laundry room, and my possessions were strewn around the garages of various friends in different parts of the city. Our first year of marriage we combined our thin possessions into the only apartment our wrecked credit scores would afford us.

In that first year of marriage, we discovered we had additional six-legged roach roommates, and they would not sign the lease or contribute to the rent. We gave away my thin mattress and paired his budget mattress and my hand-me-down bed frame as the bed in our primary bedroom. My old bubble TV sat in the living room taking up space with its "Baby Got Back" exterior jutted out toward the wall. We sat on his hand-me-down couch that started to dip into an uncomfortable U-shape we tried to ignore, and we sat on the leather chair and ottoman that in no way matched with the hand-me-down couch. My dinette set became our dining room table and my writing desk, because our small apartment did not afford me the room for an office.

We've now been married over a decade and most of the possessions we came into our marriage with are long gone, up-cycled to someone else or given away to a thrift store. We bought furniture from Ikea. Then we upgraded to Rooms to Go and Pottery Barn and West Elm outlet stores. We thrifted and perused antique shops to build the coziness of our listening room and our living room. We created a functional guest room with our hand-me-down bed frame and bought another budget mattress to rest on it. We upgraded to a faux leather headboard and bed frame. We felt so fancy until the faux leather started peeling off and falling onto our sheets.

Mattresses are only supposed to have eight years of life before they need to be replaced. This is either fact or a lie that Big Mattress tells us, but either way we believed it. We looked at our primary bedroom, our hand-me-down dressers and plastic drawers cosplaying as nightstands and decided enough was enough. We'd put so much energy into the other rooms in the house, rooms that were for us but also for guests, for family, for friends, for the Super Bowl party, for hosting during the holidays, that our primary bedroom had been neglected. Our old mattress was causing both of us back pain. We deserved better, so we decided to get each other a new bedroom suite for our anniversary one year.

We went to Macy's Furniture Gallery and walked through the showroom, peering at the bedroom furniture clustered together with tightly made beds and way too many pillows to give us an idea of how this furniture would sit in our home. We found a bedroom set we agreed on and then realized we'd need a mattress to go with it. Shopping for mattresses is such a funny thing. Lots of sitting down and feeling like your own personal version of Goldilocks. This one's too soft. This one's too firm. This one's just right. We sat down on mattresses on the same side. We sat down on different sides. We lay down on them. We bounced up and down on them. Don't scoff. We have to check for *all* possibilities.

We decided on a Casper. I'm not sure why the company is named Casper. I can't help but think of Casper the Friendly Ghost when I see the name. When the salesman came to check on us, we told him we were ready, as if he were a waiter who had returned to take our order for dinner. We felt grown up when we told him we'd take the whole bedroom suite, the bed frame, and two nightstands, and we'd take a Casper mattress. We filled out paperwork, chose delivery options, and paid more money than we'd probably paid for anything in a long time. Then we went home and waited. We slept on our old back-pain-inducing mattress until the glorious day when the new bed would be delivered.

On delivery day, we tried to work from home, but the giddiness overtook us. By the time the delivery guys arrived we had already broken down our old bed frame and headboard and given it away. We redistributed our plastic nightstands to other places around the house in need of some storage and organization.

The Casper mattress, like many mattresses of its kind, arrives to your home neatly tucked into a box much smaller than the mattress will be once opened. Like a large mattress version of a helium balloon, the mattress comes to life and takes up space until it arrives at the size of mattress you ordered. Except in our case, it meant that the process of the mattress unfolding, becoming, growing, changing, and taking shape, knocked the blades off our ceiling fan. Anyway, we ended up with a well-made, grown-up bedroom set and a very comfortable mattress. We also ended up with a new ceiling fan.

A great mattress is truly a gift that keeps on giving. Our mattress is so good we both exhale a nonsexual moan a little when we get in bed, even all these years later. We let out the relief our backs feel lying on this amazing mattress. This mattress is so nice my social calendar has to compete with it. If an artist I love is touring or a good friend invites me to an event, I have to think to myself, *Is the show or the event going to be better than my bed? Will I enjoy it at least equally to how much I love this bed?! And if not, is it really worth my time?* Who wants to go to an awkward party or a boring event when you have a bed like this at home?! Not me!

Marriage is a public thing and also a very private thing. It exists out there, at family gatherings, in the marriage stories you tell your coworkers, how you are perceived as a married person by the people who know you well and by the people who don't know you at all. And so much of marriage is a private thing. The inside jokes. The things you have laughed, cried, and argued about.

Matt and I have cared for each other when one of us was sick and in bed. We have shared the bed when we both were miserable with some flu, cold, or stomach bug. We know way too much about each other's bathroom habits when we're sick. A healthy marriage takes nurturing and an acute attentiveness.

Not just nurturing the marriage out there, the marriage other people see or experience, but nurturing the marriage in here, in our bedroom, when we brush our teeth side by side, at the end of a hard day, at the beginning of a day full of possibilities, when we find refuge in remembering we are a family as we leave the homes of our families of origin. When we return to each other skin on skin as if for the first time and as if it's been hundreds of times.

In all the years Matt and I have been married, we bought a lot of things together. But this bed is one of our proudest possessions, and it isn't for anyone else to enjoy but us. It isn't for the marriage out there, it's for the marriage in here, for us. And I love that for us. Anyway, I gotta go because even this essay can't really compete with how good that bed is.

I KISSED DATING HELLO

had the type of church upbringing that did not abide by "secular" dating rules. Dating was for marriage. Not to have fun, not to get to know someone, but to lead to marriage. This meant sometimes I watched adults in our church skip dating, going from friends right to matrimony.

After the book *I Kissed Dating Goodbye* by Joshua Harris was published in 1997, some of us were allowed to "court," which really meant dating in groups and going on dates with your boo and your family like the way Michael dated Apollonia in *The Godfather,* until you and all the church/family parties involved decided this courtship was really headed toward marriage. And I believed all that until I woke up in my mid-twenties with no dates to speak of, left my church bubble, and started spending time with people my age who maybe didn't go to church or who grew up differently from me.

In high school, I fell in love with my best friend, but I didn't know I had fallen in love with him until years after we graduated. I had a high school boyfriend I went to church with, but we were only allowed to go to church or to one of our families' homes where adults were always present to watch over us. I went on my first real date right after I graduated from high school with a cute biracial boy in my English AP class. We were pen pals during college and remained friends into our twenties, only for me to discover in my thirties he had become a Trump supporter. Yikes.

In college, I had a couple of crushes but did nothing about them because I extended my church girl résumé into being a part of a campus ministry chapter. I believed the sermons preached to me, that if I committed myself to God and to the church, a man of God would find me serving in the nursery or folding church bulletins, declare his immediate love for me, and that he would know from the small, still voice of the angel on his shoulder that I was indeed his wife. The angel would speak to him the same way the angel in the Bible had spoken to Joseph about Mary except I wouldn't be mysteriously with child.

That scenario never happened. In the years after I graduated college I spent all my spare time in church, and no one swooped into any of the church meetings to declare his love for me. I wanted to get married, I wanted to be in a relationship, but I was afraid. The thought of being in near proximity to a man I found attractive scared the shit out of me so bad I might as well have been in a horror film: *Nightmare on First Date Street: He Asked Her Out to Coffee but She Felt Too Hot and Flustered About the Prospect So She Told Him No She Had to Spend Time with Jesus Instead.*

Nobody in church was asking me out, but the more I found a social life outside of church, the more all kinds of guys were asking me out or asking for my number. I promptly told them I couldn't go out with them unless they had permission from the singles pastor, the teaching pastor, and the senior pastor, to which most of the men balked and ran, rightfully so. Bless my church girl heart.

Then I realized, I didn't want to court. I wanted to date! I wanted to at least lust lightly! I wanted to kiss and make out and cuddle! I wanted to be boo'd up before Ella Mai sang it in a song. One problem: I didn't know how to date. I barely knew how to interact with men outside of a work or church meeting.

So, I did what I normally do when I reach a hiccup in life: I read books. I read about how I could kiss dating hello. I read tips on how to become a good kisser. I read about keeping the love I'd find, about getting a date worth keeping, about keeping my boundaries in dating, and then I realized after all that reading, I'd have to actually *do* some dating.

I hoped some book sense could make up for my lack of experience and common sense. I learned from these books that dating could be fun, casual even. That despite what church (and Joshua Harris's since-lambasted book) had attempted to teach me, I could date and enjoy myself without rushing into any marriage proposals, without the permission of men whose approval was not more important than my own approval of my own life. I also learned from these books and random articles in *Cosmopolitan* that I could ask a man out without the dire consequence of a life sentence with a man who would never initiate anything else in the relationship. Bless.

My first adult date, I asked a guy at church to go see the movie *Ray* with me. He was tall and handsome and artsy. We'd hung out as friends, but when the movie *Ray* came out, I couldn't think of anyone else to see the movie with except him. He was old school. He didn't carry a cell phone so the only way to reach him was to call his home phone and leave a message on his answering machine. Whew, I had déjà vu for a second and thought I was in the plot of a retro rom-com. This happened in the mid-aughts I promise. Anyway, I called and left him a voicemail asking him if he wanted to see *Ray* that night because I wasn't sure I'd have the courage to schedule a date.

He just happened to be checking his answering machine because he was supposed to see *Ray* with a guy friend and his friend couldn't go at the last minute. He called me back immediately and let me know he was standing at the theater with tickets in hand, ready for whenever I arrived.

I had to get cute *quick*. I was living with my best friend and her husband, and she helped me whip together a cute outfit paired with a nice, flavored lip gloss, and I met him at the theater. I was nervous, but I was so damn proud of myself. I'd asked a man out. He'd said yes.

We dated a few months. We read John Steinbeck. I never thought a hill or a pasture could be described in so many different ways. What can I say, you do a lot of things when you like a person. We watched independent films. We had deep conversations. He was ready to get married. I wasn't. I told him I just couldn't see us as being more than friends and I broke his heart.

After that, I went to therapy. I did the work. I free agented my way through the dating scene. I did a dating program where I had to meet at least five new men a week. I bopped my way through various events trying to get my numbers up and give my number out. I forced myself to meet new men in the bookstore, in the grocery store, at single mingle events, and at the Atlanta Tall Club.

Yes, you read that right. Atlanta Tall Club, formerly known as Atlanta Sky-Hi Club, was a chapter of Tall Clubs International, an organization that "promotes tall awareness among tall people and in the community" at large. The rule of the Tall Club was women had to be over 5' 10" and men had to be over 6' 2".

Attending this Tall Club meeting was what I could only imagine going to a nude beach was like. In the movies, nude beaches were full of models with snatched waists and six-pack abdominals. In real life, nude beaches were mostly full of the rest of us, regaling the beach, waves, and any of its attendees with all the places our skin had decided to hang or sag. In a movie, the Tall Club would have been full of attractive basketball players and the types of sexy people you hope you end up on a random elevator with. The men looked much less like Dwayne "The Rock" Johnson and Idris Elba and a lot more like a fourth-grade teacher who wore ties and vests filled with shamrocks or pumpkins depending on the season. After someone at the Atlanta Tall Club started listing famous historical figures who were tall, I decided to use my long-legged walk to hightail it out of there.

Other than surviving the Atlanta Tall Club debacle, I enjoyed the thrill of juggling the life facts and demographics of several men for a short time, until I got tired of remembering who loved the Pittsburgh Steelers and who was from Ohio and who had a kid versus who had a dog they treated like their kid. My single mingles started to lead to some dates and I was hoping my dates would lead to a long-term relationship.

I dated a fantastic artist who was not prepared to date my abstinent ass. My high school love returned only to disappear again after some troubles with the law. I dated a tow truck driver who was formerly incarcerated. I went on sip and paint dates, concert dates, vegetarian dates. I chatted on the phone with a poet, a military man, the father of a newborn—and even a guy who claimed he worked at a car wash, co-owned a tattoo parlor, *and* went to law school. This same multi-hyphenate waited until our fourth conversation before he asked me when I would let him have his way with me, as if he were a character in an old Humphrey Bogart film. None of these dates became relationships and my friends were deeply concerned about my open-handed dating philosophy. Being an equal opportunity employer is one thing. Being an equal opportunity dater is another.

But I pressed on, because I knew the thing I needed most was the experience of dating, getting to know what I liked, who I liked, how I wanted to flirt, and what I could and couldn't stand in a relationship. I needed the time to go to coffee or a movie with someone without the pressure of deciding over a latte and a pastry whether I needed to marry this person.

I also learned some common sense: a virtual phone number to share when I first met someone until I felt safe to give them my real phone number, asking my date to meet me at our date destination rather than giving my address for him to pick me up, and always sharing the location of my date with a couple of my friends. I learned to slow down and not rush things even when I liked the guy.

I learned what I found to be attractive, and unattractive. I learned I preferred a thick man, a beefcake if you will, with thick forearms and thick thighs. I learned I liked a man I could learn things from and experience new things with, but I didn't want a man who felt his only job was to teach me things. I learned that sometimes I found a zaddy attractive, but I was not looking for a daddy. I learned that I liked to cook for my man and fix his plate, but I was not attracted to a guy who wanted to keep me tethered to home or the kitchen.

I learned the girl who felt like an unattractive nerd in high school had been a pretty nerd all along. I learned to love and like myself. I learned to enjoy my own company, to find my own hobbies and interests. I learned how to take myself out on dates and how to do things I enjoyed just because.

It was during this time in my dating life I met the man who would become the love of my life, but he wasn't at the Atlanta Tall Club or the hiking club or any of the single mingles. He was my friend and I worried my not-so-secret crush on him would betray my feelings every time we saw each other.

A BROKE LOVE STORY

This is a girl meets boy kind of story, but mostly this is a broke love story. A tale of two artists meeting as they were both trying to rebuild their lives. I was a broke artist who'd quit my good corporate job to pursue my artist career, only to end up in debt and back in a dead-end job. He was a year into single life after divorce, having recently moved back to his hometown of Atlanta to start his life again.

We met at a church, even though I swore up and down I was done dating guys I met at church. I had performed poetry during the church service and after service a tall, red-headed white man came to the merch table and bought a CD. He introduced himself as Matt but told me some of his friends called him Opie on account of the red hair and all. He asked me if I did other poetry events around the city, and I did what any single person would have done in the early aughts. I told him to add me on Myspace.

You might be like, Myspace? What's that? Oh nothing. Just a little website where young Gen Xers and elder millennials learned HTML code and how to prioritize the visibility of our friends via a profile Top 8. If this is unfamiliar to you, ask one of your friends who was a latchkey kid or uses the phrase "keep it real" unironically or still says "word" or "crunk." Trust me, they'll know.

We became Myspace friends, and I invited him to a poetry event I was performing in at a coffee shop. He showed up wearing a sky-blue Kangol that matched his shirt. His jeans baggy enough to tell me he went to high school in the 1990s just like I did. He had this slow, Southern gait about the way he walked, a rhythm to the way his shoulders dipped whenever he took a step, and it made me want to walk with him anywhere. He played it cool. Told me he couldn't stay long because he had another event to stop through. I nodded that I understood. We chatted awkwardly. Me. I was the awkward one. I had not taken in how fine he was when we met at the church, how talking to him was making my skin warm and making my heart beat fast.

I wanted to go to dinner with him. I wanted to sit across the table from him and a tealight candle, eating bar food or French pastries or sushi. It didn't matter really. As long as we were talking and laughing and trading new facts about each other. I wanted to know where he grew up, what music he liked, if he liked me.

We kept running into each other, on the side of a stage, or in a greenroom at some event. Who was this man and what was he about? I used my superpower of pulling conversation out of just about anyone. I became a young, inquisitive, dating investigative reporter. He was a musician, saxophone his main instrument. He worked at the church where we'd met. He deejayed sometimes too.

I had just started hosting an open mic and invited him to deejay. This was Atlanta after all. Everyone was a deejay or a music producer, but you couldn't tell if they were actually good at it until you could see them in action. I'd already dated at least one guy who couldn't stop listening to the beats he made while we were in his car headed to dinner, who couldn't stop talking about that beat he almost put on T.I. I figured if Matt was terrible at deejaying, it was just an open mic. Sixty-five percent of the people performing at an open mic range from beginners to wack anyway, so it wasn't a big risk.

He showed up to my open mic with his turntables and impressed me, the crowd, and my artist friends. We became friends. He became the permanent deejay for my open mic. I invited him to hang out with me and my friends. Then I had an idea. I wanted to do a show combining spoken word and deejaying. I found a studio where we could work from and asked if he was willing to build a show with me. I told him I didn't have money to pay him, but I thought if we built a good show, I would do my best to get him paid. He agreed.

The day of our first studio session I went to the grocery store, Publix, and started filling up my basket with food. I figured the least I could do was make sure he had some food to eat during our four hour studio session and possibly enough food to take home with him. I picked up two Cuban sandwiches from the cold deli section, two bags of Cool Ranch Doritos, two small bottles of sweet tea, plus some food for myself. I wasn't sure what kind of sandwich he liked or what his favorite chip was, but I assumed he would like Cool Ranch Doritos. Who doesn't like Cool Ranch Doritos? Especially if you're of a certain age. Or spent a summer passing all eight levels of *Super Mario Bros.* and finally saved the princess. Or knew the theme song to *Full House* by heart.

Cool Ranch Doritos were one of the highest levels of

cafeteria currency in elementary school, right next to Gushers. You would nearly trade your whole entire lunch for one bag of Cool Ranch Doritos, especially if your parents didn't allow you to eat Doritos or if Doritos weren't in your family's budget. Those Cool Ranch Doritos were slowly whispering my secret to my artist friend, Matt. I liked him at the highest level and therefore he deserved the kind of chips you'd trade a baloney sandwich, Lay's, an apple, and a juice box for. But neither one of us could hear the message those Cool Ranch Doritos were trying to tell us.

One night the open mic went badly, by my definition. I'd invited an artist to perform who was used to performing in church, and he opened his set by asking the audience, "How many of y'all love God?" and one of my open mic attendees tugged on his beard and said, "Depends on which God you talking 'bout, bruh?" After the open mic, I told Matt I wanted to debrief. I don't know what I expected him to say. Maybe that he'd call me on the way home? But he did me one better.

"Let's get something to eat. I know a place we can go. It's open late and the food is great. Let's go to Café Intermezzo," he said.

He might as well have said Paris, or the top of the Empire State Building, where Meg Ryan met Tom Hanks in *Sleepless in Seattle*, or the New Year's Eve dance where Billy Crystal confessed his love to Meg Ryan. Damn. I have a lot of love fantasies that involve Meg Ryan movies.

Café Intermezzo was a den of romance. When I was in college this was where you took someone if you wanted to get serious. If you were ready to tell your friends y'all go together. It was a dimly lit, French-inspired bistro and dessert haven. The coffee list was longer than the food menu. The tables were a little larger than a laptop, forcing you and your wanna-be-lover to lean in to eat, drink, or make out. I'd never had a date take me to Intermezzo, but I knew it by reputation. In college, $7 desserts were a big splurge, so if a guy invited you out to Intermezzo, it meant he'd saved up his work-study money. For broke people trying to get out of debt and make a new way in their lives, Café Intermezzo was just affordable enough.

"Sure," I said as my voice cracked like puberty decided to wildly revisit me in my late twenties, "I'll meet you there."

I pulled myself together before I walked in the door. *It's not a date until he says it is*, I told myself. There he was, sitting at a table the size of a throw pillow, the shadow of the tiny tealight flame flickering across his gorgeous face. We drank fancy cocoa and coffee. We talked about art and religion and music. He didn't flirt with me once. I was too scared to flirt with him, so we continued in a friendship that had some feelings hiding underneath it.

Later that summer, Matt and I met up at a rap show and watched one of his favorite rappers have a meltdown onstage. The show was not well organized or well promoted. The show was in fact so bad I decided not to stay, and Matt decided to leave too. When we got to our cars in the parking lot, I said, "I'm hungry," and he said, "Let's go eat."

We met up at this empanadas spot in East Atlanta Village. We both ordered the small amount of empanadas we could afford. I never knew the flaky crust and delicious filling of an empanada could have a truth serum, but I decided I'd had enough of all this friend posturing when I was slowly falling in love with him. We talked about our past relationships and what we wanted from a future relationship. The conversation spilled over to the phone after the check was paid and we were headed home. I decided enough was enough, I needed to go ahead and tell this man I had feelings for him. I decided to ramp up my courage.

"We're both adults. Our friendship can handle this," I said

as my words and feelings circled the runway of finally telling him the truth.

He understood where my long preface was headed. He admitted he found me attractive, and he wanted to see about us, to see if we could be an us. A few days later we met up for our first official date. By this time, he'd seen me in my sweatpants, T-shirt, and flip flops, and I'd seen him in his summer mohawk and his threadbare shirts with cargo shorts. For the first time I was thinking about what I was wearing and if he would think I looked good.

Our first date was at Orient Express, an Asian fusion restaurant shaped like a train. Half of the restaurant served hibachi and half of it served Chinese food. The waiter led us to the hibachi side and we both gasped when we looked at the cost of the menu items. We switched over to the Chinese food side, where we might find some things we could afford, and ordered two stir-fry dishes we both were too nervous to eat. I squeezed in next to him on the same side of the booth.

We ate burgers all over Atlanta and fell in love over cheap pizza slices. We boo'd up at free hip hop and jazz concerts, shared donuts and wing combos. We met up at Chili's even when we weren't hungry just to have a few minutes to share an order of Southwestern Egg Rolls on our lunch break. Falling in love with Matt made Applebee's taste like it deserved a Michelin star. Looking in his eyes across the booth at a Waffle House with two plates of scattered, smothered, covered hashbrowns felt to me like the type of thing James Beard should award.

We drove through our city, listening to Outkast rap about liberation, wood grain steering wheels, fish and grits, the dungeon, singing the blues, Headland and Delowe. We drove down Peachtree Street, kissing at all the stoplights.

It's been almost fifteen years since then: a wedding, a

honeymoon, a dog, three addresses, four career changes, two hospital stays, three of the biggest paydays of our careers, performing together in four countries and twenty-nine states. We rebuilt our lives and we are still building. We enjoy the starched linen and unique eats of fancy restaurants, but more often than not we find ourselves searching for the hole-in-the-wall in whatever city we find ourselves in: eating Chicago hot dogs, New York pizza slices, Los Angeles tacos, Nashville hot chicken and fish, and North Carolina, Tennessee, and Texas barbecue.

Sometimes we return to the broke roots of our early love and take our date night to an Atlanta wing spot. I order barbecue wings and lemon pepper split and he orders hot wings with ranch on the side. We look across the table at each other as he sips on a root beer and I sip on whatever peach drank the wing spot has to offer. We see the people we were when we met, new to each other with a few of life's bumps and bruises to show for it. We see the people we are now, the things we've survived, how we have held each other's hands through things we didn't know at the time how we'd survive. How I need my emotional support hand sanitizer on the table at all times. How he needs enough ranch and ketchup to swim in. How we have learned to love so many versions of each other now. How important it is to us to love each other and like each other too. Still. I sip his drink like it belongs to me. He finishes up the fries I have abandoned. We remember we are living the good life.

ON BEING IN AN INTERRACIAL MARRIAGE

My husband and I entered our interracial relationship in the year of the iPad, the signing of the Affordable Care Act, the debut of *The Walking Dead*, and the eloquence of Antoine Dodson's poetic quote, "Hide yo' kids, hide yo' wife, and hide yo' husband."

Other than Matt I have only dated two other white guys. I met Austin on eHarmony and we made the unfortunate choice to meet up at the Atlanta History Center for our date, a history center full of, unbeknownst to us, Civil War exhibits. Yeah. Yikes. After one too many Confederate flags and stories of Confederate soldiers, we decided maybe grabbing something to eat was a better plan. I had a thing about getting in the car with a man if I didn't know him well. So even though Austin offered to drive us both to a nearby lunch place, I told him I'd feel more comfortable if I could drive myself—and then I had a fantastic idea. We could walk. The lunch place wasn't that far. Weren't we in some kind of rom-com where the weather was pleasant for a walk at any time?

We got to know each other really well on that walk. I learned that my estimations of time and space are completely inaccurate. I learned Austin had a condition where his health needed to be monitored by an apparatus that hung from his neck. I don't know what the numbers meant on this device. I just know it kept beeping and Austin was really sweating and turning a bit red. I learned my weather estimations were also inaccurate. It was not a breezy day for a walk through the city. It was hot as hell, and as Austin's breathing became shorter and shorter I wondered, Was this going to be the first date I'd ever have where I sent my date to the hospital?

Austin and I made it to a little taco place. The air-conditioning and the ice water helped him. We may or may not have ridden a cab back to where our cars were parked. I felt I'd already endangered him and maybe shouldn't endanger him further by going on any more dates.

The other white guy I dated I met at a place I'll call White Community Church: a large set of churches where lots of white people of middle and higher income went. White Community Church had a singles gathering, so I took one of my Black women friends, Camille.

"Let's go get us a Ty Pennington," she said.

So, we went to the White Community Church single mingle and met two white guys who wanted to take us on a double date. My girlfriend had snagged herself a short, redheaded pilot and I had bagged a tall, lanky brunette. Wait. Are white guys with brown hair considered brunettes or brunes?

We decided to salsa dance for our double date. You might wonder why we decided this. I question this choice to this day. Anyway, we went to the salsa club, and it turned out the salsa instructor had to skip out on our lesson at the last minute. It was too short notice to find a replacement, so the salsa club turned on some salsa music and invited everyone to dance. Except my friend and our two dates had no idea how to dance salsa.

My girlfriend and her date danced a bit but mostly talked. But my date? I'll give it to him, he was adventurous and unafraid of being embarrassed. He made up his own dance to the music and held my hand and offbeat twirled me around for several songs. It was entertaining how much he had no care or concern about how terrible of a job he was doing while he danced. We lasted like this for about an hour, and after some conversation and drinks we decided our double date had done the best it could.

He walked me to my car and I offered to drive him to his. But I forgot I had been listening to Kanye West's *Late Registration*. Right as I cranked my car up, Kanye and The Game yelled, *"That's that crack music! That real Black music!"*

At first, I felt embarrassed, but then I thought about it and I let it play. I figured this is what it's like hanging out with me, or being in a relationship with me, and if this is a dealbreaker we might as well end before we start.

We chatted awkwardly and immediately started talking about if we'd ever dated outside of our race. I didn't bring up that the only other white guy I'd dated may or may not have had a health crisis on our first date. That seemed like it might be an overshare. But I asked him, "Would your parents be okay with you bringing a Black woman home?" and he said, "Oh no. Absolutely not."

Neither one of us knew what to say after that, so I dropped him off at his car. We said pleasantries to each other, but both of us knew we would never speak again. By the time I was driving back to my apartment, Brandy was singing, "I always knew that one day they'd try to bring me down," and I wasn't sure if she was talking about racism or offbeat salsa dancing. Either way, Brandy was right.

Matt and I became newlyweds during the time of the Tan Suit. Beginning an interracial relationship during the Obama era was a combination of the United Colors of Benetton, the movie *Something New*, and the dreamy effect of all that talk of hope and change and progress. We talked through the issues of each election, local and national, about politics, about our thoughts on race and history with the limited language we had at the time.

By the end of 2016 and the election win of a racist reality star to the presidency, the wind was shifting away from the illusion of progress and more toward Black Lives Matter, resistance, and protest. I tried to imagine what life would have been like if Matt and I had met in the year of Beyoncé's *Lemonade* instead of in the year of Lady Gaga's VMAs meat dress.

What would it have been like if we'd met now? In these political times? There would have been a lot more questions to ask. There would have been a lot more vetting a Black woman would have to do to consider dating a white man.

Maybe there would have been a seventeen-page application before any dates could be established. The application could include questions about favorite heroes, web search history, previous addresses, work and relationship history. A checklist to see if they've read and watched certain books and movies, including *The New Jim Crow*, *13th*, *Selma*, and *Origin*. A psychological test of reactions to words like "fragility" and "privilege" and "white supremacy." A professional social media scouring for Confederate flags, alt-right references, retweets of Joe Rogan, and excessive posts about *The Wire*.

Once a candidate passed the written application, an interview would be conducted before any dates could be scheduled.

The interview committee consisting of people the Black woman is in community with. Maybe someone Black who says "Grand rising" every morning, maybe one Black person who's read multiple books by Audre Lorde and bell hooks, one Black auntie who has most conversations with her hand on her hip, one Black uncle who calls other Black men "Doc," or possibly including one white person who is like Jacob's character on *Abbott Elementary*. This committee will complete three rounds of interviews of the potential white man date in question and determine if he is eligible for even a coffee date. If a white man passes the rigorous interview stage and the Black woman he's asked on a date approves, he will be granted a coffee date no longer than ninety minutes. The Black woman will consult the committee for a post-date debrief, where she will determine if a second date is permissible between her and this white man. And at this rate it could take a decade before the relationship could grow from casual dating to long-term.

But Matt and I didn't have our meet-cute during the time of the envelope fiasco between *Moonlight* and *La La Land* at the Oscars, Kendrick Lamar's Super Bowl, or Doechii's Tiny Desk. We instead navigated our lives and marriage during the rise of the #MeToo movement and the Black Lives Matter movement, the engagement and marriage of Prince Harry and Meghan Markle (the Royal Interracial Couple), a global pandemic, the uprisings of 2020, the gutting of DEI, and the rollback of many civil and human rights.

To be in a healthy marriage requires tending, cultivating, intentionality. The willingness to do the work of growth and healing, as an individual and as a couple. To be in a healthy interracial relationship requires all of these things, plus the commitment from both partners to continue the work of antiracism: including the tending, the uprooting, the planting, the disentangling.

Because Matt is in my life, I have watched way more Adam

Sandler movies than I ever thought I'd see, and I know way more Beastie Boys songs than I ever thought I would. He has listened to more India.Arie and Jill Scott than he ever imagined. When we go to hip hop shows we love to stand or sit in the front. When we go to comedy shows we never sit in the front. This is also a hidden rule of being in an interracial relationship. Every now and then a song by R.E.M. or The Cranberries will come on and I'll watch Matt sing his heart out. He knows if I were to ever become a deejay, my deejay name would be DJ Beyond Say because I'd only spin Beyoncé songs and I'd take no requests.

To be in an interracial relationship is not to be the poster child of progress. For us, it's just two humans, traversing life and the world, the beauty and the terrible parts, with a willingness to try, to learn, to unlearn, to grow, to fight for change, to change ourselves. It's also two people telling each other the hip hop lyrics and 1980s jingles we can't get out of our heads. How else would we know if it's Friday night and the mood is right?

FINDING YOUR COUPLE CHARMING

Finding couple friends is hard. Finding a partner isn't always an easy find either. But once you've found your person, you may desire to hang out with other partnered ass people. Finding another couple both you and your partner get along with can be a long and winding journey of awkward double dates, insecure meetups, and shaky small talk until you find your Couple Charming.

Sometimes you have a friend who has a boo, so you and your friend take your boos out for a double date. You may discover you love your friend, but you only tolerate their boo because you love your friend. You watch their boo interject things into the conversation that don't make any damn sense. You find you, your friend, and your boo have much better conversation when your friend's boo goes to the bathroom. You will never tell your friend you hope they break up with this person. You will never tell them you would rather they become amicably divorced co-parents than make you suffer another awkward Super Bowl party. But when you're home alone you light a candle and charge your moon water and hope and pray your friend decides to get into a relationship with someone you actually enjoy kicking it with.

Sometimes your friend has a boo that you *love*. You enjoy the shit out of them. You would hang out with them without your friend. Every time you see an ad for a ring you nudge your friend to go ahead and make this engagement happen. But then you get the call. Your friend and their boo have decided to call it quits. You know your loyalty is to your friend, but you contemplate for a second if you and your friend's ex need to meet for coffee and closure, to talk about all the future plans y'all had that have now been ruined by this breakup. You look longingly at their social media profile right before you unfollow, thinking about that one party dish they made, that one drink they mixed so well. Then when you're home alone you light a candle and charge your moon water and pray to the dating gods (which are Will Smith's Hitch, what's her name from *How to Lose a Guy in 10 Days*, and a Black relationship expert you saw on OWN) that your friend's next boo will be equally as good as or better than the ex you actually liked.

Then there are your friends who are in a well-established couple. They've been married or living together longer than *The Office* had seasons. You meet at the house of a friend, at a work function, at a random event and strike up an interesting conversation. You agree to meet at a bowling alley, at a "new" restaurant, or heaven help us at one of your homes for a dinner party.

It's all fun and games when you first meet. You laugh at each other's jokes; you find their stories about their jobs or their kids or their extended families hilarious, but now you're cornered at a booth of a restaurant that serves New American food and you've realized there's one thing about your couple friends you can never know at a first meeting: a relationship temperature check.

You don't find out until the appetizers have arrived that one of them doesn't find the joke their partner always says about them funny at all. One of them wants to split the entrée, the other one thinks it's ludicrous to split food for any reason. One of them thinks Ludacris is one of the greatest emcees of all time, and one of them can't get past Lil Wayne not even being in the conversation.

Sometimes your double-date night turns into fight night, where you and your spouse are eating fried calamari or black garlic edamame across from two people who you are now not even sure like each other. You were really looking forward to dessert but now your partner is pinching your leg under the table and sending you secret texts, letting you know y'all can stop at the store and get dessert after you leave this terrible date.

I wish there was a relationship-a-lizer where a couple could breathe into an apparatus and you could gauge the percent of shit their relationship is in: 30 to 48 percent, healthy couple; 49 to 66 percent, slight amounts of toxicity; 67-88 percent, the relationship is in danger, girl; or 89 to 100 percent, one DM away from a big breakup. Then from there you could decide if you want to hang out with a couple who may very likely use your couples' double date as an opportunity for free relationship "counseling."

Before the antipasti or primi course, before you have buttered the warm bread in the basket at the table, before you've had time to dip it in the very important olive oil and herbs, the couple across from you has started throwing various scenarios at you and your partner. They are asking you questions like, "Is that fair?" or saying things like, "Maybe you'll understand this," or "It's always something with this one." I never know how to respond to this. I just wanted to eat my pasta in peace, so I try to bring solutions to the double date.

"Now, Lisa, why did you cancel Hulu without talking to Sharon? You know how much she loves a true crime series. Sharon, you were supposed to talk with Lisa *before* you bought that new TV. Not everyone wants a picture frame around their television," I'd say while eating a piece of asparagus.

"Eddie, yeah, your kids just may not be fun to hang around, which is why your wife's trips to the store always take longer than they should. And, Angela, yeah, your kids just may not be fun to hang around, which is why Eddie stays in the bathroom so long," I'd say while eating off my husband's plate.

You end up becoming a counselor and a referee, all while trying to enjoy some roasted brussels sprouts and crab bisque.

There are a lot of variables about double dates that will be out of your control. Consider me your awkward double-date survival guide and consider these things before you put that double date in your shared calendar:

- Pick a restaurant you really like. If you have to spend dinner watching two people argue, you should at least get some good food out of it.

- Choose a date that involves an activity. Go bowling or apple picking or cow tipping or race car driving. It's harder to fight in bowling shoes or out in a field with cows.

- Let a date night that becomes a fight night give you a different lens from which to see your partner. Maybe your partner's incessant talking or loud burping or early morning chipperness isn't so annoying after all. Especially after you've spent the evening with two people who turn your conversation on your hip hop top five into a discussion of reasons they *know* the earth is flat. Maybe you'll realize although your partner can be annoying, their annoying is an annoying you can live with.

- You could also discover just how irritating you've been to other couples on double dates. You may realize in hindsight that performing improv or giving tongue kisses at the table is not what other couples want to experience on a double date. Even if you think you and your partner have a spot-on impression from *Coming to America*, now that you've had some bad double dates, maybe you'll think twice. A bad double date can be a personal learning experience too.

Matt and I have had our fair share of bad double dates with new friends, old friends, and coworkers, double dates that ended awkwardly because we didn't know queso would bring up a huge communication issue or because we didn't realize our friends were looking for us to take a side in the fight they'd been repeating for years. But sometimes double dates have a happy ending. Matt and I have gone on an escape room double date where no one argued or cried. We've found other couples to try new restaurants and walk through life with. We've gotten good advice from couples whose relationships had been in existence about as long as we'd been alive. We have walked with our couple friends through unemployment, having kids or deciding not to have them, navigating co-parenting and divorce, and deciding what constitutes a "couples'" TV show. We are learning not only how to be good double-date people but how to be good couple friends.

Wouldn't it be great if there was a double-date matching app? I want double dates that are fun but not argumentative, interesting to talk to but not only interested in talking about themselves. If they have kids, I don't want the whole date full of kids' stories. If they don't have kids, I don't want to spend the whole dinner talking about how terrible kids and parents are. I don't want to be proselytized, preached to, or propositioned. I just want to eat a nice dinner, see a good movie, do some fun activities, and go home and say, "Man, they were cool, weren't they?"

RELATIONSHIP RULES

've been married for over fourteen years, and I still like my husband. My husband is pretty easy to like. He's a fun, funny, easygoing, sunny-side-up morning person who knows how and when to leave me to my mid-morning attitude and pessimism that I refer to as realism. Between my previous dating life and now married life, here are a few things I've learned about relationships:

1. Always Have a Bathroom Prepared for Number Two

My husband and I are past the cute time of dating or first living together where there is fear and awkwardness around going number two. I pooped in my own bathroom and clogged up the toilet while we were dating, and as my then-boyfriend he plunged the toilet until it flowed freely. I went boo boo at his parents' and my now husband plunged the toilet until it flowed freely. I did a stinker at my acupuncturist's office, and my man did his best to fix the plumbing.

Moral of the story is, if there's no crying in baseball, there's no room in marriage or a long-term relationship for being timid around shits. Poop is going to happen. It happens to the best of us. It happens to the worst of us. It happens to all of us.

We've been married a long time, but we still try to preserve the sexy, which for us means not making a habit of farting outside of the bathroom. I really typed "farting" for my husband because I know it makes him laugh. I was raised not to say farting. I was raised to say pass gas, and poot on special occasions.

Keep a good spray in your bathroom. You should do this for the times you offend yourself, but you should definitely do this before your boo comes over. Keep a plunger in the bathroom in case you have a boo like me whose poops clearly like to clog up a toilet. If it's safe to do so in your home, keep a candle and a candle lighter or one of those wax melt things in your bathroom. As beautiful, sexy, cute, adorable as your sweetheart is, they gon' stink it up sometimes. Wouldn't you rather the smell of peppermint or lemon balm or whiskey bourbon snow or whatever you can pick up from TJ Maxx than the smell of your boo's boo boos?!

Always have at least two extra rolls of toilet paper. Bonus points if you like to have a few wipes hanging around. You never know what bathroom situations can arise.

Help your boo help you.

2. Do What's Best for PMS

You may have a partner who menstruates and if so, lean in close. I don't care if you saw blood coming out of them or if they acted that exact same way the last time it was close to their period. *You* don't bring up their period. *You* don't say things like, "You must be on your period." If they don't mention a period *say nothing.*

If they do mention a period, *you* ask things like, "Is there a snack I can get you? Salty or sweet? Want some company? Would you rather be left alone? Here's the remote, let's watch whatever you wanna watch. Need any period products? Sure, I can go pick that up for you." *That's it.* If you love them, this is your job now. I don't make up the rules. Okay, in this instance, I did *but the rules still apply.*

Once my period starts, I become ravenous. I amble down the street like Dawnn Lewis's character Cheryl in *I'm Gonna Git You Sucka*, making anyone in my path squeal like she did Damon Wayans's character Leonard. One plus to being married a long time is my husband knows the vibes. I sequester in our room, he brings me takeout from our favorite burger place, and I slide the empty tray out with the satisfaction Shug Avery felt after trading Mister's burnt biscuits for Celie's delicious soul food in the movie *The Color Purple.*

He hands me the remote and listens vaguely to Kyle and her sister fighting on *Real Housewives of Beverly Hills*, or me yelling at the TV while watching *90 Day Fiancé*, or me watching *When Harry Met Sally* for the fifty-'leventh time and marveling at it like I've never seen the movie before. He has chocolate, a heating pad, and my favorite blanket, and he tiptoes backward out of the room to protect his neck as The Wu said we should.

Offer comfort and control to your period-having partner. Give them chicken wings, Tofurkey, Cheeto balls, or whatever they ask for. It'll pass. At least until the next period shows up. You have my blessing in the meantime.

3. Know Which Side of the Bed Is Ours

If I knew then what I know now I would have put it in my vows. I would have told my husband in exchange for marrying me he was giving up his personal space. Maybe he should have seen it coming: me asking to sit on the same side of the booth as him on our first date.

All these years later his side of the bed is our side of the bed. Every piece of food or drink he has includes a portion that is mine for the taking. His side of the couch is our side of the couch. And if he is working on his laptop on the couch, I am nuzzling up to him because something about his eyes on the laptop means his eyes should be on me.

This isn't my fault. That man shouldn't be as good at snuggling as he is. He shouldn't have such a good palate and order such good food and drinks. *I can't help it everything he has is delicious and warm and nice and good.*

4. Keep Your Weird Pet Names to Yourself

Baby, boo, sweetheart, these kinds of pet names are fine. But when you start edging into the Big Daddy, Kitty Cat territory, *pause.* I'm sure most of the people who love you and love the way your person loves you want you to be cute and in love. But if your boo thang is Sweet Peaches to you, *we don't want to know why.* Keep that to yourself.

Know the limits of being disgustingly in love. People might think it's a bit much, but they want good things for you. They just don't want to picture you and your boo in any kind of compromising position. *In any position. At all.*

I have been privy to some out-of-hand pet names. My husband and I work hard to not be those people. We've slipped up a couple of times, and one of them may or may not have been in a work email. But let's focus on the point here! If there's an inside voice and an outside voice, then there are inside pet names and outside pet names. Stay aware of your location! Your friends and family wanna know you love your baby boo, *not* that you call them Candy Shop at home. *Read the roooooooom.*

I AM NOT OFTEN ASKED WHAT I THINK THE SECRET TO A LONG-TERM relationship is. These seem to be questions reserved for relationships that have passed the twenty-year mark or survived at least two recessions. But when I say how long Matt and I have been married I can see people's eyes doing the calculations. Fourteen years is a long time to be at a job, at one address, or a fan of a sports team. The truth is there isn't really a secret. It's more like a series of intentions, thoughts, and considerations that will be different for each relationship, a tender balance that requires the consistent willingness of both partners. For ours, it's a combination of keeping indigestion in mind before any sexual activity, understanding *Real Housewives* is to me what the NBA is to him, learning to make room and space for each other, for our boo boos, for ourselves.

WHY I'M NEVER GOING HORSEBACK RIDING AGAIN

'm done with horseback riding. No shade to those of you who love this as an activity. I wish you well. I don't want to be near a horse ever again. I have put in my time. I've had some amazing experiences. And I've had some experiences that are the reason why this is not a thing I'm doing anymore. One of my friends was talking about how she really wanted to go horseback riding with her husband. As soon as she said it, it brought back all these memories as to why I will no longer be participating.

I went horseback riding for the first time when I was about eleven years old. My sister Makeda had just been born. I had always wanted a sister but my assessment of the stages of development was a bit off. When I envisioned having a sister, I imagined we'd be close in age, ready to play Monopoly, read Ramona books, and play freeze tag, but my infant sister was unable to do any of these things.

After my sister was born, so many people came over to see the baby. Everyone was interested in someone who couldn't talk to them, couldn't really entertain them, couldn't do anything but cry and go to the bathroom in a diaper someone else had to clean up. The people really visited our home for this.

When my mom's friend and fellow nurse Ms. Dara came over, I opened the door, pointed to the baby, and said, "She's over there."

"I'm here to see you," she said. "I'm here to pick you up, and we're going to spend the day together."

I smiled the biggest smile I could find and hurried to get dressed. Ms. Dara was a beautiful Laotian woman with a sharp haircut and a no-nonsense attitude. I spent the day hanging out with Ms. Dara and her friends, and we went horseback riding. It didn't matter to me what we did. I was just excited somebody was paying attention to me.

Her friends and I arrived at the horse stables. My horse's name was Chestnut. The stable hands helped all of us into our saddles and we began our ride slowly down the trail. On either side of the trail there were vines of poison ivy, and Chestnut started eating them as a snack. I didn't know a whole lot about poison ivy, but I was concerned. Is my horse trying to harm himself? Is poison ivy poison? I mean, it has *poison* in the name. Is my horse going to literally poison himself eating poison ivy?

The stable hands took a large bag of Chex Mix, cut the top off, put Chestnut's muzzle in the Chex Mix bag, and led Chestnut back to the stable, ending my ride early. That was my first experience horseback riding. Maybe that should have told me I should have let it be my first and last experience.

MATT AND I ONCE TOOK A TRIP TO BOTSWANA TO PERFORM AT A gala to celebrate the medical professionals there. The doctor who invited us set up our accommodations at a lodge on an animal reserve that offered safari on horseback as an excursion.

This was probably one of my best horseback riding experiences. The zebras and giraffes let us get closer to them on horseback than they would have if we had been on our two legs. Growing up in the States, I had only seen zebras and giraffes in books and at the zoo, so I was amazed at the vivid colors of their fur, the enviable length of their eyelashes, how majestic they were in person.

A couple of years later, Matt and I were invited to Costa Rica. We had some friends who we also worked with at events, and they took couples' trips. One year they had all planned a trip to Costa Rica, and one of the couples at the last minute couldn't go.

We knew three out of the four couples who were on the trip. The couple that couldn't go gifted us their lodging slot. All we had to do was pay for flights to Costa Rica. We had just enough frequent-flier miles for one of us to have a free ticket, so all we had to do was pay for the other ticket. Come through two for one!

We arrived in Costa Rica, and we were staying at a house that used to be a bed-and-breakfast. The dining room, the living room, the kitchen were all outdoors. Part of these areas were covered, but it was still outdoors. There was a pool in the shared living area, and there were four bedrooms with en suite bathrooms, so each couple had their own private space. The bedrooms were the only areas of the house that were fully indoors. Once we stepped outside of the bedroom, we were outdoors, which for the most part was great, but according to how much mosquitoes like me, maybe not so much.

In preparation for the trip, we read so many things about the excursions: ATV rides, horseback rides, cooking demonstrations, and coffee tastings. Whenever we ate breakfast there, I noticed the corn tortilla was thicker than what I knew most corn tortillas to be. Instead of them being used to wrap things, like a taco or a burrito, they were put on the bottom of the dish, and for breakfast, you might have black beans, cheese, and eggs to top your tortilla. One of the excursions I had read about included a horseback ride with a Costa Rican coffee tasting and a quick lesson on how to make Costa Rican tortillas.

By the time we went into town for our ATV excursion, I was confused about which excursions were offered where. When we returned from our ATV excursion, I saw a place to sign up for a horseback ride the next day. The description looked so similar to the horseback riding with coffee tasting and cooking demonstration, I thought they were the same thing. So, Matt and I paid to go horseback riding the next day.

The following day, we met back at the place where we started our ATV excursion and a young teenager picked us up in a little hatchback and drove us to our horseback ride. I know a little bit of Spanish, and so does Matt, enough to conversationally get by. We arrived at a house with a small horse stable in front. I asked our guide in very broken Spanish, "Are we going to learn how to make tortillas?" He spoke in Spanish, and the older woman of the house went in the kitchen, made tortillas and served coffee, both delicious.

"Will she teach me to make these?" I asked our guide via small amounts of words in Spanish and hand gestures.

He spoke again in Spanish to the older woman, and she shook her head. As a person who respects boundaries, I nodded and kept things moving, wondering if there was someone else who might teach me how to make the tortillas as noted in the excursion description. Matt and I mounted our horses, and our teenage guide led us out on a slow horseback ride. The concierge excursion list had described the horseback ride as providing a view of the beach and ocean, which we could not see so far on the trail.

We kept going and going and going. I was getting so nervous I kept saying English phrases to the translator app mixed with one of the few phrases I knew en español. "Cómo se dice, 'How far are we from the beach?'" I asked our guide via the translator app on my phone. Before I could find out, a torrential rain poured down on us while we were on horseback. Given the type of road we were on, there was hardly any place to go. We had to ride for a while until we found a little awning to stand under until the rainstorm passed.

"Cómo se dice, 'How far are we?'" "Cómo se dice, 'Are we getting close to the beach?'" "Cómo se dice, 'Can you just take us back to where you dropped us off?'" He turned us around. We rode the horses back to the older woman's house, and another teenager drove us back to the meetup point in that little hatchback. It was then I realized I hadn't signed up for the right excursion at all. No wonder the woman of the house scoffed at the idea of me asking to come into her kitchen! We thanked our guide and headed back to our villa, drenched.

When Matt and I got back to where we were staying, we realized everyone else was leaving in the morning, but our flight wasn't leaving until very late the next night. We looked through all of our excursion links and found the one I'd been looking for. We decided to try one more time before we headed to the airport for our flight and scheduled a horseback ride, coffee tasting, and tortilla cooking demonstration for the following morning.

The next morning, we waited outside of the villa and our

guide picked us up in a car, stored our luggage in his family's offices, and drove us out to their family farm. He told us what he loved about his home country, the beauty of the hills, the plants, the people. We tasted pour-over coffee from their farm. The women in the family showed me how they made those amazing tortillas, how they formed the dough, the way they cooked them in a curved stove over a fire, and with their permission I recorded a video of their cooking lesson.

After that we began our horseback ride to the beach with new guides, the same beach we were told where Beyoncé and Jay-Z filmed the music video for "Drunk in Love." If I'm in a place where Beyoncé was, do I feel like that probably makes us friends? Yes. Of course.

As we were riding, our guides told us different sounds to make or commands to give to the horses, how to use the reins to slow down or speed up. These horses were trained to stay together as a pack. If one horse started going faster, the others followed suit. I couldn't get my horse to slow down. If the other horses sped up, my horse did too, and quickly.

My horse was running at a frightening pace and felt out of control. I got so scared, I started sobbing on the horse. Our guides freaked out, and I could hear them asking Matt, "Es tu esposa?" and Matt telling them, "Si, mi esposa." Our guides were very sweet and kind, and one of them took the reins of my horse and led my horse alongside his. We finally arrived at our stopping place on the beach, and it was beautiful, a view of sun and sky as far as our eyes could see; a beach made of sand and crushed seashells. I had stopped sobbing long enough for our guides to take a picture of Matt and me kissing each other while we were both on horseback.

So much of marriage is navigating the uncontrollable variables of life: health, family, career, horseback-riding excursions. It's finding ways to think of "tu esposa." Sometimes the vulnerability of marriage is enough to make you so scared it makes you cry. It takes patience and being willing to go slowly and take your time. Marriage is mistakenly signing up for the wrong horseback ride and then going on the right horseback ride and then crying on the horseback ride while showing your spouse support on the horseback ride, especially so you can get a kissing horseback-riding picture for social media.

We rode our horses back over to the stable, retrieved our bags, and headed to the airport. I decided that was my last horseback ride. I rode Chestnut on horseback while he ate poison ivy. I got rained on, on horseback. I sobbed on horseback. I rode horseback in three countries. It was time to go out on top. I put in my time. I gave it a try. I hope the horses live well.

I WAS RECENTLY WITH A FRIEND OF MINE HEADED TO A CONCERT IN downtown Atlanta. Like many cities, we have horse-drawn carriages for people who feel like that's romantic. I don't. My husband never has to worry about me asking to feel like Cinderella in a horse-drawn carriage. I don't want that. I would like to be in a car. Let my transportation be horsepower driven, not a horse-drawn carriage. My friend and I walked by, and the carriage horses had blinders on, but the horse kept turning to look at us.

We turned and walked the opposite way. I'm not dealing with this. I don't care. I'm not doing that. The man in charge of the horses said, "Why y'all scared? Y'all scared?" Yes. Yessir I am. Also, it turns out, Beyoncé and Jay-Z filmed "Drunk in Love" in Florida, not Costa Rica, but at least the coffee and tortillas were good.

PART 6

"A WHITE REFRIGERATOR? PLEASE PUT YOUR SHOES ON. LET'S FIND YOU A HOME," AND OTHER THINGS I LOVE ABOUT POP CULTURE

DEAR TV SITCOMS

Dear TV sitcoms
I am mad at you
You raised me wrong
Restricted me to your twenty-two-minute plots
Your seven and a half commercial breaks
Your forty-five-second catchy theme songs
You made being an adult look so easy
Easy like getting dressed for work in the morning
Coming home right after the commercial break
It turns out sitcoms don't have time for an eight-hour
    workday
Easy like being a writer while being able to afford to live
    alone
In New York
With a closet full of Manolo Blahniks

Easy like raising five kids while you work as an attorney
And your husband works as a doctor
And you are somehow always home when the kids get
    home from school
And you can afford to host celebrities and take amazing
    vacations

You made me believe that grown women
Are randomly wearing sexy panties every night
Like in real life our bras ain't raggedy
Like in real life we don't all keep a drawer of reliable
    granny panties

You made love look so simple
Simple like two *Perfect Strangers* who met at *The Office*
In the first season they're just *Friends*
An episode or two later they are *Married . . . with Children*
Like in real life some of us don't find ourselves *Living
    Single*
Long after our attempts to create a *Modern Family* have
    turned up empty
Sometimes when *Girl Meets World*
These are the years where you wonder if you gon' find
    love before your *Girlfriends* become *The Golden Girls*

You made me want to get aboard *The Love Boat*
You made marriage look like arguments and foot rubs and
    pillow talk and matching pajama sets
Had me all in my feelings
All Martin and Gina
And Lucy and Desi
And Jim and Pam

And Kevin and Winnie
And Dwayne and Whitley
And James and Florida
And Synclaire and Overton
Like I was in Natalie's with my boo
Like it's the last two minutes of *New York Undercover*

You had all the answers to drugs or bullying
You told me just say no
The more you know
No means no
Don't talk to strangers

You even tried to help my abandonment issues
When you said, "After these messages . . ."
You actually came right back

But we don't all get to escape the hood of West
    Philadelphia
We don't all have a rich Uncle Phil or a rich Aunt Viv
For the record, my loyalties always lie with the first
    Aunt Viv

Some of us watched our hood lives turn into *Good Times*
Couldn't imagine ourselves a college boy or a college girl
Until we saw ourselves on *A Different World*
We liked *Family Ties*, but we needed *Family Matters*
To remind us how much Black families matter
Families like the Jeffersons and the Parkers and the
    Sanfords really do exist
Why all these years later we still need real-life hashtags to
    explain why

Everybody Loves Raymond but *Everybody Hates
    Chris*

You can't fix the world's problems in twenty-two minutes
Maybe that was never your goal
Maybe all you wanted to do was reflect life back to us
No matter how much we scroll or stream
Binge-watch our newsfeeds
Use our thumbs more than our mouths to say what we
    really mean
We're all just looking to find a norm
Hoping to walk into our favorite spot and hear them say
    our name
Like they did Norm

Maybe you did raise me right
You rolled the credits so I could get back to my real life
Find my own theme song
Create my own plot
Do the best I can with my own God-given time slot

AN ANGRY BLACK WOMAN PLAYLIST

The Hulk had the permission to get so angry he turned green, but Black women have not been given the permission to be angry. When my mom would get angry, she would say her chest felt hot and her cheeks felt as if steam were rising from the sides of her face. I didn't know what she meant, until I started to get angry too. Whenever Black women speak directly or matter-of-factly, we are accused of raising our voice or being aggressive. It's as if the mythical Angry Black Woman parades around town, bigger than life; more villain than hero, throwing her hips and attitude into every building or person she passes by.

I have been a part of many underground Black girl meetings, a quick Zoom, a side FaceTime, a gathering in the corner of a conference, where the topic of discussion was a scenario in which a Black woman we knew had been accused of being the

Angry Black Woman. Sometimes the term itself was never said, but words like *combative* and *attacked* sliced through the air like darts in a work meeting, landing directly in the heart, and marring the reputation of the Black woman in the room.

In these conversations with friends, colleagues, and co-workers, we prepare the talk. We discuss even tone. We reread each other's email drafts before they are sent to review for any sentences that could be viewed as curt or short. We role-play potential conversations for upcoming meetings. We take deep breaths together. We do what feels like a thousand things to remove the sting of being perceived as an Angry Black Woman. We do everything we can to not be perceived as or accused of being an Angry Black Woman in the first place.

My therapist once told me I was holding back my anger. Which of course made me angry. She told me I needed to learn how to process it, to express it. She encouraged me to feel anger itself, not to scoot anger to the side too quickly for what could be viewed as a more palatable emotion underneath. She reminded me anger and rage are valid and proper responses to many things in life, being pissed off is not worse than the shit I'm pissed off about.

So, I did what I do when I want to express an emotion: I made a playlist. Mixtapes and playlists had carried me through a lot of feelings: falling in love, breaking up, struggling to go to the corporate job I hated, feeling insecure, and wanting to find my confidence. I decided to create an Angry Black Woman playlist.

Beyoncé's *Lemonade* felt like a great place to start, since the initial teaser images for the visual album included Beyoncé wearing what I could only gather were *Set It Off* cornrows. As soon as I saw Beyoncé rocking the straight backs, I knew she was mad as hell. When Beyoncé released the video for "Formation," I should have known what was coming by the fact that she was standing on top of a cop car submerged in water. This was more than, *Oh how fun! Beyoncé has hot sauce in her bag!*

By the time the *Lemonade* visual album was released it became clear the hot sauce she kept in her bag was not just the condiment you put on collard greens but also a baseball bat you could use to bash the headlights of your enemies. In the "Hold Up" video Beyoncé is dressed in a whimsically ruffled marigold dress with long, blond-kissed waves of hair, and she takes a baseball bat from a child to the rhythm of an island-tinged beat. Beyoncé starts bashing the windows of a car, which we learned from Jazmine Sullivan could be a cathartic healing practice at the end of a relationship. I added "Hold Up" and "Bust Your Windows" to my playlist.

Beyoncé Giselle swings a home run on the fire hydrant, causing water to flood into the street. She flounces through town with a skip and a smile and all the pissed-off feelings in the world. She relishes her anger and lets it flow through her, bashing windshields, checking her image in a security camera and then bashing that too. I learned from being raised by a Black mama you should steer clear of a Black woman who has become so angry it makes her smile or chuckle. Make room. Give way. Let her cook.

By the time the visual album takes us to "Don't Hurt Yourself," Beyoncé is whipping those long straight-back cornrows over her shoulder while donning a fur, a bralette, rings on every finger, an ankh chain, and a pair of leggings in the parking deck the "Beat It" dancers abandoned. Even Jack White was basically there to play his notes and sing his lines and stay the hell out of Beyoncé's way. Hurt me? Hurt yourself! I added this song to my playlist too.

Megan Thee Stallion convinced me I could be "Not Nice." Kelis gave me the permission to sweetly sing to a 1990s R&B beat and then yell out my hate and rage along with her on

"Caught Out There," which many of us refer to colloquially as the "I Hate You So Much Right Now" song. I began to embrace my rage with inspiration from the royalty of Lady of Rage, who would have been the talk of the Bridgerton ton with her afro puffs and stuff.

Next, I added a song by this young woman from the Bronx who immediately asserted her dominance by letting a "little bitch" know she would not be A, B, C, D, E, effed with by introducing what should be one of the Pantone colors of every year, "Bodak Yellow." By the time Cardi B arrived at letting these hoes know if she sees you and refuses to greet you, you could take that as a sign that she's not your friend and has no pleasantries to give you, I was hip hop head nodding.

When Cardi articulated the importance of mental health and dental health by letting us know she used her newfound money for jewelry, stuntin' on these hoes, and to get her teeth fixed, I appreciated the note that it is not cheap to get one's teeth fixed. It was as if Belcalis Marlenis Cephus, our Bodak bard, our urban poetess, grabbed my ear by her lengthy coffin fingernails and inspired me to channel my anger by yelling *"Bitch!"* as loud as I could right along with her. It turns out this word is not just a favorite word for Too Short.

My next destination on my Angry Black Woman Playlist took me to Rico Nasty. How could I not add Rico as she sweetly screamed to me, if I was in a "Rage" I could "Let It Out," I could tell anyone "STFU" who deserved it?! If I could choose having a big sister, I'd choose Rico Nasty because I know she wouldn't have let anybody on the playground get away with messing with me. If you ever get caught in a situation where you need someone to plead your case, call Rico Nasty. If somebody does you wrong and they need to be read for filth, let Rico Nasty do it. If your partner does you wrong, let Rico Nasty accompany you to the coffee y'all are having for "closure." She'll convince you they never deserved you anyway and make them afraid to text you "wyd" or "you up?"

I could dance to a booming beat and be angry as hell! Leikeli47 persuaded me to relish having an "Attitude," because of PMS, because of America, because somebody touched my hair without asking. Which led me right to the seat at the table Solange built with her song "Don't Touch My Hair," a healing anger if you will. Solange reminded me sometimes anger is soft and tangible, deep breaths and clarity, I could count it all joy *and* have the right to be "Mad."

Rihanna reminded me all outstanding invoices, net 15, net 30, net 60, net never, be damned, they better have my money, through rain, sleet, or snow. They better have the money they need to pay me and the money they owe me for equal pay and reparations.

My playlist ended maybe where it should have started, with Nina Simone, who after the bombing of the Sixteenth Street Baptist Church in 1963, which resulted in the killing of four little Black girls and the murder of Medgar Evers, penned "Mississippi Goddam." At first Nina Simone was singing about Alabama, but over the years she swapped out the place in her song to Memphis, Selma, and Watts as justice movements happened in other places in the 1960s. Nina Simone's riotous and riveting piano reminded me it's not only okay to be angry about how America has me so upset, I could also give a good "Mississippi Goddam" for every injustice, for every act of violence, for every inequity. She reminded me it's also powerful to be angry.

Black women have been understandably angry for a long time. We have sometimes swallowed our anger until our bodies could no longer hold it, silenced our anger until our voices could no longer speak, sacrificed our health and wellness because we were afraid to express our anger. Even in the face of our anger being dismissed and minimized, we have channeled that anger into protest, community organizing, music, visual art, dance, comedy, theater, and activism.

Black woman anger is personal and private and public and communal. It is not a thing to be ashamed of but instead a thing to be channeled and expressed. In action. In creativity. In art. In activism. When we cuss. When we yell. When we vote. When we speak. When we have our say. When we cry. When we laugh. When we sing. When we rap. My Angry Black Woman playlist and all the angry Black women before me have reminded me it can be good to be an Angry Black Woman.

WHY I TAKE A BLACK WOMAN DAY OFF

When I worked in corporate America there were two types of time off: sick time and PTO (paid time off). I'm here to submit the same way there are third spaces, there should be a third type of time off: Black Woman Day Off.

Every Black woman should receive an unlimited amount of Black Woman Days Off. This is to address the intergenerational trauma of those of us who are the descendants of the enslaved Africans, and this time is also meant to acknowledge the anti-Blackness all Black folks of the diaspora face. A Black Woman Day Off can be taken at the Black woman's discretion. Especially if you work with the kind of white people who are always listening and learning, sending thoughts and prayers. You need a Black Woman Day Off from those people.

Reasons to Take a Black Woman Day Off

- The day of the Super Bowl, to celebrate Janet Jackson Appreciation Day

- The day after the Super Bowl whenever a Black performer does the halftime show

- The day after any Black person dies due to injustice

- The day after anyone prominent and Black dies

- Dr. King Day

- Juneteenth

- The day after the Grammys, if there were exceptional Black performances

- The day after the BET Awards, if there was a tribute or an award given to a Black artist you love

- The day before you attend the concert of a Black artist

- The day you attend the concert of a Black artist

- The day after you attend the concert of a Black artist

- The week of your Family Reunion

- The week of Essence Festival

- The weeks all the Black people head to Martha's Vineyard

- HBCU Homecoming even if you didn't attend an HBCU

- Beyoncé Day: A day reserved for when Beyoncé drops an album unannounced, announces a tour, or announces she is selling bees or honey. Or if you need to buy tickets to her tour, or if you attended her tour. If you watched *Homecoming* or *Lemonade* or Beyoncé Bowl and need a day to think about it.

- When you have an appointment with your Black dentist, doctor, therapist, hairstylist, nail artist, jeweler, or mechanic

- On braids preparation day

- On the day you get your hair braided or your locs tightened

- The day after you get your hair braided or your locs tightened, in case you have a headache

- A Black Reading Day, where you read a book by a Black author

- A Black Listening Day, where you listen to Black music or a Black podcast or a Black elder

- A time to lay your ass down and do nothing because being Black is enough. Being a Black woman is enough. Being yourself is enough. Being human is enough.

THE KEY OF G

I was born of tambourine and handclap
Foot stomp on old wooden church floors
Learned to love a sound that came straight from James
   Brown
Not the Godfather of Soul
I'm talking about James Brown, my father
Whose soul is earth, wind, & fire
Whose eyes were *shining stars for me to see*
Earphones bigger than six-month-old me
Placed around these little ears
So I could hear a slice of *what my life could truly be*

My grandma used to say
"Your daddy can play piano by ear"

Which meant his heart could hear what his fingers could
    interpret
His mother taught him to play in the key of G
And he passed that blessing on to me

No matter how many times old Ms. Patterson reminded
    me to practice
I couldn't focus on the keys
I left the piano notes alone
Picked up a pen and a microphone
I learned to live by ear
Listening to the bass blasting from my twenty-dollar
    boom box
Like ripples of water through the floor of my bedroom
The only keys I pressed were record and play
To capture my favorite song off the radio

This poem is for the quiet storm
The request line
The first time I understood the magnitude of *Shhh don't
    talk just listen*
For my first real date
How we slow danced to "All My Life" with his hands
    around my waist

For the old holiness hymns my grandmother taught me
For my mom buying me The Boys' first LP
When I believed Hakeem would marry me
This poem is for Trey
Who taught me Black Thought called me *a queen named
    Amena*
For that bootleg cassette of the Fugees

And my first taste of L. Boogie
This is for my college roommate
Who lent me six of Coltrane's greatest hits
I never did give her back that CD
This poem is for Daniel with the brown freckles
Who sang me the words to "Under the Bridge"

One day, a young person might ask me
"Where do samples come from?"
I want to sit them down and tell them the truth
That real music is this special dance instruments and
    lyrics do
One day Baby you'll find somebody special
You'll do that dance too

I want you to listen to John Coltrane and Miles Davis
I want you to know a 45 is more than a loaded weapon or
    a terrible president
That needles and records go perfect together
Maybe in life I'll only get my sixteen bars
I hope my eyes are shining stars for you to see
To remember how to live by ear and play in the key of G

EVERYTHING I NEEDED TO KNOW IN LIFE I LEARNED FROM *THE REAL HOUSEWIVES OF ATLANTA*

The start of 2018 began about as badly as 2017 ended. Between the end of one year and the beginning of the next, I experienced an overwhelming amount of loss, both personal and professional. This turned me into a real-life version of Mellie from *Scandal* season 4, wearing a bathrobe all day, eating potato chips for breakfast, and eating fried chicken anytime I damn well pleased, but instead of this causing me to push for gun reform as it did Mellie, it inspired me to watch a pop culture juggernaut from the very beginning: *The Real Housewives of Atlanta*.

The Real Housewives of Atlanta, created by Princess Banton-Lofters, first aired in 2008. I began my *RHOA* journey wearing my raggedy bathrobe and jumping quickly into the lives of Atlanta socialites, athletes' wives, and single-mother entrepreneurs. Watching the show ten years after it first aired was a perfect time capsule of original noses, baby doll tops, liquid leggings, ruffle dresses, and ill-fitting wigs. I had the opportunity to see the gworls before they were fully aware of themselves.

I saw the beginnings of the mythology of She by Shereé. A time when we had no idea everyday people took pole dancing classes. I watched Kim Zolciak pretend to be a singer, have her life funded by a mystery man named "Big Poppa," and *gasp* confess that she was a Black woman in a white woman's body, in a time before some white folks were listening and learning. But are they listening?! Are they learning?!

I watched Nene Leakes search for her biological father and advise her castmate to "close her legs to married men." I listened to the sound of the gworls fighting, arguing, asserting themselves, and sharing shade with each other whenever I had trouble sleeping. I quickly caught up through season 10 and was ready when season 11 aired in the fall of 2018.

Since then, I have been a die-hard fan of *The Real Housewives of Atlanta*. My grandma had her "stories" and this was mine. My grandma concerned herself with Nikki and Victor and Mrs. Chancellor from *The Young and the Restless*. I concerned myself with whether or not Chateau Sheree or She by Shereé would ever be completed. Having a set of "stories" is my heritage. Like my grandma, I didn't just watch my "stories" for entertainment, I watched for lessons I could learn about life. I decided if I had been cast as a Real Atlanta Housewife my tagline would have been: "Play spades, but don't play with me."

Here are the things about life I learned from *The Real Housewives of Atlanta*:

- **Shift your own wig before you shift the wigs of others**

  Shereé gave Kim Zolciak's wig what should be considered a strong tug, but Shereé claimed she could not understand why this was such a big deal when she merely "shifted" Kim's wig. Do unto others as you would have them do unto you. Listen without judgment. Focus on your own wig. Worry about yourself first.

- **Sometimes it is better not to call Tyrone**

  Erica Abi Wright, also known as Erykah Badu, also known as Baaaaag Laaaaady, also known as Can You Call That Otha Otha Bass Player, is a known sage for many Black women. She sang the trials and tribulations of having a good for nothing man in your life and the strong need to call his homeboy Tyrone to help him get his shit. But when Nene and Shereé decided to fight while drinking glasses of wine, it was Tyrone who was the cause of the fight, and they both felt the other one was good for nothing. Assess who is actually the Tyrone in the situations of your life. Evaluate if Tyrone should actually be called or if it is Tyrone who should also pack his shit and leave your life.

- **Always have a freaky friend**

  Kandi Burruss gets the honorable mention here for being the freaky friend of *The Real Housewives of Atlanta*. If every hero should have a theme song, everyone should have a freaky friend.

Kandi's freaky curriculum vitae is lined with proof she's the friend you wanna go to for advice on freaky behavior. Kandi took *the lies the lies* Phaedra told and made an event out of it. People paid money to experience "The Dungeon" that never even existed in real life. Kandi had a YouTube channel called Bedroom Kandi, and then she parlayed this into a line of sex toys with the same name.

Get you a freaky friend who will hand out remote-controlled sex toys on a couples' trip and laugh while each partner jumps every time they have a Beach Boys moment and feel the vibration. Get you a friend who will bring a sex swing to the bachelorette party. Who will randomly book a male stripper who is known for his big membership and I'm not talking about a church congregation!

- **Manifest your dream life with the same power as Linnethia Leakes**
  It is a thing of the chicken and the egg whether you become a rich bitch and then announce you are a rich bitch, or if you meditate upon being a rich bitch and then become one. But just this one time, listen to the Instagram gurus who are trying to sell you their e-courses. Let them influence you. Manifest the life you dream of, but more than that, listen to Linnethia Leakes, who gave us such powerhouse self-help meditations as "I said what I said" and "We see each otha." You too can become a woman of wealth or however you define rich. I hope one day Nene Leakes writes a dissertation called "Bloop: The Importance of Onomatopoeia."

- **Do not surround yourself with ashiness**
  As Black women, we know and understand the importance of not being physically ashy but remember ashy is not just a state of skin, it is also a state of mind. Our great poet Porsha Williams inspired us all to say farewell to ashiness. Turn to your neighbor and say, "Bye, Ashy." Moisturize your skin. Moisturize your heels. Moisturize your life.

- **Always come home to yourself**
  Luther said, "A house is not a home," but a house can become a home. Even if it takes nearly a decade to complete said home. Even if completing the home rivals your ability to produce a fashion show without fashions. Home is not confined to Chateau Shereé or Moore Manor, whether or not your basement is finished or if you have a white refrigerator. Home is inside of you and who gon' check you, boo?

IN THE YEARS SINCE I STARTED WATCHING *THE REAL HOUSEWIVES OF Atlanta*, the show has changed and so have I. Instead of Shereé shifting wigs, Nene proclaimed, "Bye Wig!" Marlo tried to say hello to her wig line but was eclipsed by newly minted drum major Kenya stomping through her wig event yelling, "Kenya Moore Hair Care!" Porsha became an activist and Kenya *ate*. Not her outfit but crabcakes and left the girls hungry on a girls' trip. Marlo invited the ladies to a peace retreat where there was no peace, and She by Shereé finally debuted fashions before spring, summer, September.

The show has featured singers, Olympians, influencers, real estate moguls, and tech titans. There have been weddings and divorces, baby showers and graduations, deaths and disappointments, fights and faux apologies, and I have been watching through it all. I thought self-care would arrive to me in deep meditative breaths with sound bowls and mantras, and sometimes it does. But sometimes self-care arrives in sitting down with a snack just in time to watch a Real Housewife of Atlanta wear Balenciaga to just about anything, read or prepare to be read, say something that will become a meme, and/or impart a life lesson to last a lifetime.

CELEBRITIES I'VE MET
AND MISTAKES I'VE MADE

There are a few times in my life where I've met celebrities. Many of these meetings are without autographs or photos because I tried to play it cool cool cool. But there are a few celebrity meetings where I did not play it cool. Like meeting Brené Brown and introducing myself as her cousin because we share a last name. Or meeting Chris Tucker and asking about his relationship with God because my next question was going to be "Will you marry me?" Here are a few of my favorite celebrity sightings:

Strength, Courage, Vegan Food, and India.Arie

I have loved India.Arie's music since her first album, *Acoustic Soul.* I own most of her albums—not just streamed them, owned them, either bought them on CD, or bought them and downloaded them when that first became a thing.

In my early twenties, I was working my second job after college graduation as an administrative assistant to a Black woman event producer named Pam. This was my second favorite job I've ever worked, next to the job I do now, as a writer and a performer. Pam produced big fundraising galas for nonprofits. For one of these events, she booked India.Arie to perform. I was super excited. But I also knew I needed to be professional.

The night of the gala, it was my job as Pam's assistant to check on all of the talent, make sure everybody had everything they needed, and complete whatever tasks Pam requested. I went down to the greenroom and discovered although India's rider told us she was vegan, no vegan food was provided via catering.

India told us about an Indian restaurant she loved nearby that had wonderful vegan food. A committee member and I commandeered a limousine in front of the venue, rode quickly to the restaurant, ordered as many vegan dishes as we could, rode quickly back to the venue, and ran in our heels to get the food to India and her team.

At the end of the event, Pam walked up to me with a Swarovski crystal award. With a knowing look in her eyes, Pam handed the award to me and said, "Why don't you go and give this to India?"

I thought to myself, *What if I never see India again? What if this is my one moment?* I gave India the award and told her we appreciated her for being a part of the event. She was kind and so excited to get the award because of how it was made. She told me she loved crystals, and she was very excited to receive a Swarovski crystal award.

"India, I really love your music, and I listen to it all the time. One of my favorite songs is 'Strength, Courage & Wisdom.' I listen to it on the treadmill."

As I described this to her, I started doing a running motion, trying to demonstrate to her with my whole body what I do on the treadmill, and I had the gall to start singing at her.

"I get on the treadmill and I'm like, '*Strength, courage, and wisdooooom it's been inside of me alllll along.*'"

India was very kind and gracious. She chuckled and said thank you, and thankfully I found enough strength, courage, and wisdom to shuffle away from her before I further embarrassed myself.

Meeting Common and How I Could Be Converted into a Groupie

In my mid-twenties, I wrote as a music journalist for a local media outlet: part career inspiration and part hustle to get free concert tickets. Common was coming to town as a part of John Legend's tour, shortly after John Legend's album *Get Lifted* had been released. I reached out to John Legend and Common's publicist to see if I could schedule an interview. She replied to let me know she received my email, but then after that, no response.

Common put on a show. He rapped. He freestyled. He breakdanced. He performed almost all the facets of hip hop. After his set, Common went to the merch area for a meet and greet. I got in line to try one last time to see if I could get a quick interview.

Common was wearing a yellow polo shirt with a Kangol to match. When I got up to the front of the line, I looked in his eyes. Everything professional I could have had in my mind left me. I looked so deep into Common's eyes, I was transfixed by the dotting of freckles across his face.

I saw my possible future. I could become a groupie. That could be my job. Forget journalism. Forget being a writer. I could be a character in my own personal *Almost Famous* movie, going city to city trailing the tour bus.

When I played basketball and volleyball in high school, we used to have breakaway pants we wore to the games. When it was time to play, you could snap those pants off from the waist because we wore shorts underneath to actually play in. That night I wished my then-bootcut jeans were breakaway pants, because I would have pulled at the waist, snapped those pants off, and given them to Common.

Professional Amena managed to speak up and I introduced myself.

"Hey, Common, nice to meet you. I really wanted to get an interview with you, reached out to your publicist, and never heard anything back."

Common took a pause for a minute and then he looked into my eyes and said, "That's okay. We'll see each other again, won't we?"

I don't know if you've ever experienced your body feeling like it is going to spontaneously combust from the inside out. That is exactly what I was feeling at the end of this conversation. Is this a thing that Common probably says to everyone who's in line at his merch table? Maybe. Did I care about that at the time? No. He might as well have been asking me to marry him or to commit to a life of being a groupie as far as mid-twenties Amena was concerned.

Missy Elliott, Love Poems to Jesus, and Being Directed by Robert Townsend

In 2005, Missy Elliott launched her own reality show called *The Road to Stardom* and auditions were held in Atlanta. I was a budding spoken word poet looking for opportunities to get onstage, so I downloaded the multi-page application, gathering as much video and audio as I had of myself performing, and went downtown to wait in line for my audition. Bad news is I didn't make the show. Good news is the show brought me one of my favorite reality TV catchphrases and brought us a star we would also come to know even better much later.

When Missy had to decide which artists would leave the show, they'd have to meet her on the tour bus of the show, and if they weren't up to par, Missy would tell them, "You're going places, just not with me." I love the sharpness of this phrase, the accuracy. The phrase just works whether you're talking about a relationship, a slice of pizza, or an ill-fitting bra.

Secondly, the winner of that show was Jessica Betts, whom we now know as a music phenom and wife of Niecy Nash-Betts. I particularly have such warm feelings about the way they announced their relationship to the world. It was like the relationship version of when Beyoncé debuted her self-titled album. I went to sleep one night and there was no Beyoncé album. I woke up the next morning (*I woke up like this?*) and not only had Beyoncé dropped an album, but it had apparently broken the internet and rearranged the atoms in the universe. The announcement of Jessica and Niecy's relationship and wedding also broke the internet, made me love love even more, and made Valentine's candy taste sweeter. The producers of Missy Elliott's *The Road to Stardom* decided they were going places, just not with me. But The Bettses decided they were both going places and they were going together.

Now, after getting rejected for this show, a door closed but a window opened. A call for auditions went out for a TV show featuring college and college-age performers, to be shown on a new network founded by Will Packer. I took my already prepared packet of information about myself to this audition and was selected to be on the show.

The part they didn't tell you until days before the shoot is that we were going to be directed by Robert Townsend. Yes, you read that right. *Meteor Man* Robert Townsend. *Hollywood Shuffle* Robert Townsend. *The Five Heartbeats* Robert Townsend. Black filmmaker, Hollywood disruptor, the creative innovator himself was going to direct my performance of one of my poems I wrote at a little coffee shop table.

Robert Townsend's demeanor was warm, friendly, and professional. He worked with each of us individually to get the best performance out of us. The poem I auditioned with was a poem about God, disguised as a romantic poem. I'm not sure Robert Townsend knew it was about God at all. He seemed to pick up mostly on the romantic language in the poem. He directed me to let the audience and the camera into the intimacy of the words. I may have run my hands down a wall as a romantic gesture for the piece. All I'm telling you is somewhere in the archives of one of Will Packer's production companies is footage of me, looking like I'm performing a poem about an irresistible man, but it's actually a poem about Jesus the Christ. One day, I hope Robert Townsend and I can have a laugh about this in a Delta Sky Club or on the set of some new comedy I'm writing, and he's directing, a show about a girl who accidentally falls romantically in love with God and all the awkwardness that ensues.

But the awkwardness doesn't end there. After each artist filmed their performances, we each needed to film a title sequence, so we were divided up into groups of three or four for this shoot. My team of four was instructed to meet at an urban set of train tracks in Atlanta. The other performers did great with their title sequences. They peeked around tree trunks with a smile. They looked mysterious and contemplative as they walked near the train tracks.

When it was my turn to peek around the tree trunk, I noticed the producer giving me additional direction. As the day went on, the other performers were sent home as they had already gotten enough footage of them. The producer tried me near the train tracks, in front of a cool-looking brick wall. No dice. Finally, the producer said, "Is there a monologue you know that you could perform and we could shoot for your title sequence?"

"Yes! I know a monologue!" I said.

There was only one monologue I knew by heart. I had performed it multiple times for my friends. The scene in *Lean on Me* when Mr. Clark and Ms. Levias go to Kaneesha's mom's basement apartment on Halloween night to convince her mom to let Kaneesha move back into the house and to help her with her schoolwork at home because Kaneesha is smart and is the pride of *sings* *fair Eastside praise they name praise thy naaaaaaame.*

Kaneesha's mom opens the door for Mr. Clark, Ms. Levias, and a sorrowful Kaneesha. Mr. Clark shares his frustration that Kaneesha's mom was such an active parent in elementary school, why would she leave Kaneesha hanging now?! Ms. Levias tells Kaneesha's mom Kaneesha has a "spark" and they want to keep her engaged in her education. Kaneesha's mom tells her story about having Kaneesha as the result of a teenage pregnancy, about losing herself in the process, about becoming an addict and then getting clean.

Camera zooms in on Kaneesha's mom and then begins the part of the monologue I focus in on. Except, I hadn't memorized the monologue because I had such a strong appreciation for the dramatic tones of the moment. I found this monologue hilarious, and I had been doing my best comedic impression of Kaneesha's mama for years.

"I don't want *huh* to see me like this *no more* . . . Why would I wanna get rid of *huh*? I love *huh* more than myself."

We discover via montage as the students and teachers of Eastside High prepare for standardized testing that yes everybody is somebody and that Kaneesha's mama loved *huh* enough to help *huh* with *huh* homework.

I performed that monologue with my standard comedic take and not only did it bomb instead of getting me laughs on laughs like it did with my friends, but the producer and crew decided they were done for the day. They would find a way to cut a title sequence of me from all the bad takes we'd filmed earlier.

Lessons learned:

- Don't sing to a singer if you can't sing. It's like baking bread for a baker. Or making candles for a candlestick maker. And yes, I do love nursery rhymes.

- Breakaway pants can be lingerie too. I said what I said.

- Don't write romantic poems about God. They really get lost in translation.

- Focus on writing, instead of acting. Don't memorize any more monologues. Please.

THE LEGEND OF THE LATCHKEY

Growing up as a child of the 1980s was a time full of imagination, mainly because our parents weren't around a good bit of the time. We played make-believe, freeze tag, and video games. We wrote stories, songs, and raps. We played outside for extended periods of time with no one to check on us. There was a special group of us who had been entrusted with the key to our home to let ourselves in after school while our parents were at work: the latchkey kids. I was eight years old the first time my mom gave me a key of my own.

As an adult I spent years working in customer service, and one of the key tenets of good customer service is setting the expectations. Be clear with the customer about what they can expect to receive or the limitations of the product they are choosing to buy. Setting the expectations properly is a way to ensure customers don't have to come back into the store with unnecessary questions or call back into customer service because they need help.

My mom was a genius at setting the expectations. At the beginning of my fourth-grade year, she handed me a key to our apartment, pressed it tightly into my hand like a church mother giving you a dollar for your birthday, and let me know the rules.

"I'm giving you a key to this apartment. When you get home from school you are gonna open *my* door and lock *my* door behind you. I will put some snacks and juice boxes in the bottom right cabinet. After school you can have a snack, and you have thirty minutes to watch TV. Then, you better get that homework done. And if I find out anybody crossed the threshold of this apartment . . ."

Then it would go silent, as if I was to assume the worst would happen to me since she didn't even give me an inkling of what my punishment would be.

I was a rule follower, so I pretty much did what she said. This was before parents had the technology to see you via Bluetooth camera. I believed my mom had Bluetooth eyes and that somehow, she could see exactly what I was doing while she was finishing up work. Some of my friends didn't have moms who left snacks for them after school, so I'd tell them I could pass them a hot Pepsi or a cold Capri-Sun if they sat on the apartment steps and let me bring it out to them. They understood that a follicle of their hair could not be found in the apartment if they wanted to see me at school the next day.

The 1980s was a prime time for snacks. This was before we studied the sugar on labels or asked a lot of questions about how things were made. Gushers? Fruit Roll-Ups? These were delicious and nutritious snacks made from fruit juice. And yes, one percent of fruit juice counts. Natural fruit flavor? Also counts. We drank Tang. I mean the astronauts drank it, why shouldn't we?

With snack and juice box in hand, I turned on the TV. It was a glorious time for television. All of those great cartoons with fantastic theme songs to watch. *DuckTales* and *Gummi Bears* and *Care Bears*. Apparently bears were having a *time*. I watched my thirty minutes of television filled with kid joy and then I did my homework, and usually right before I finished, my mom was home from work to make dinner for me and check my homework before I went to bed.

By the time I was in fifth grade, I felt like a latchkey professional. I was doing pretty good at keeping up with the key (losing Mom's key was worse than losing your parking ticket in an expensive parking deck). My friends knew the drill, so they didn't press me about trying to come inside the apartment, plus I think they were also scared of my mom. Now that I was one year older, I was starting to watch big kid television and afterschool specials, warning me against strangers and reminding me to say no to drugs.

My mom also had started to build a nice VHS tape collection. Some of which were official VHS tapes and some of which were homemade VHS tapes. And by homemade I mean Mom put a blank VHS tape in the VCR and pressed record when one of her or one of my favorite shows or movies was on. Some of you may be reading this and wondering what the hell is a VHS or a VCR. These days they could be medications you heard the side effects of, or they could be a special political party, or an online community of guys named Victor. Either which way, all of these are nowhere near what a VCR is. A VCR was a big metal box that housed big rectangular tapes that you slid into the VCR slot to play VHS videotapes. This was how I was able to watch the *Care Bears* countdown until I could say the movie to myself from memory if I had any trouble sleeping.

My being a year older did not increase my TV time. I still had thirty minutes to work with between after school and when my mom got home, so some days I opted to watch part of a VHS tape instead of watching television.

One day after school I found a tape that was made for children by a guy named Eddie Murphy. He wore a red leather outfit, sang songs, told jokes, and told funny stories. His children's program was called *Delirious*. I wasn't sure what that word meant, but his program seemed like it would be worth my thirty-minute viewing time. He said a lot of things I didn't understand, but I liked his impressions of James Brown, Stevie Wonder, and Michael Jackson. And I liked how much the audience laughed at and with him.

Then he started to talk about the ice cream man and I knew I was watching the right show because the ice cream man was very important to me at the time. I too had begged my mom for dollars and quarters and chased the ice cream man down the street of our apartment complex. My favorite order was a Nutty Buddy or a Strawberry Shortcake bar. Sometimes our ice cream man sold chips and soda, and if so, I ordered a bag of Funyuns and a grape soda. I felt so seen that Eddie Murphy talked about the ice cream man during his children's program because I loved the ice cream man too.

I was a very obedient child, so for three weeks straight, I watched thirty minutes of Eddie Murphy's *Delirious* and then I did my homework. Dear reader, Eddie Murphy's *Delirious* is in fact not for children. A lot of the problematic and questionable content went over my head, but yes, I watched a foul-mouthed, problematic stand-up comedy routine for three weeks as a fifth grader and it changed my life. I didn't know it was problematic, and I wasn't sure it was foul-mouthed, but I decided not to repeat any of the words he said just in case. The moment I saw Eddie Murphy walk out onstage in a red leather suit in front of an audience so massive it sounded like a roar every time they laughed, I knew I wanted to do that someday. He had nothing but a stool, a microphone, and his stories, and that's all he needed to captivate an audience. Right then I knew I wanted to tell stories onstage when I grew up.

After this, I watched a video of Whoopi Goldberg's one-woman Broadway show. I watched videos of Robin Williams, Billy Crystal, and Richard Pryor doing stand-up. I learned what they were doing was called comedy and I announced to my mom and grandma I wanted to do it too. For years I forgot about this pronouncement of my little kid self. As I got older, I moved on to wanting to be a banker because I thought I'd get to keep all the money, or wanting to be a gynecologist because I thought my job would be to talk to women all day. I was a grown-up in my thirties by the time I remembered I'd always wanted to tell funny stories.

Eddie Murphy was twenty-two when he filmed *Delirious*, fresh off a meteoric rise that began with his hilarious stint on *SNL*. He made a lot of problematic jokes, I later learned when I watched *Delirious* as an adult. He also had what looked like an s-curl, so in hindsight he might have done a few things differently if he knew what he knows now. The thing I remembered most is how he captivated a crowd by just being himself.

Like Eddie, I've had some missteps, wearing shirts with ribbons, being narrow-minded, and wearing winter shoes in the summer. I spent the first part of my career in conservative church spaces, making the art people wanted me to make, doing the performances that were expected of me. I did my first solo-ticketed show the year I turned thirty. I brought my new poems and new stories to a small crowd, and I got so nervous I forgot to say the poems and instead told all my funny stories back-to-back. Since then, I keep rediscovering my funny, which is really rediscovering the joy of what it's like to tell a story and know that people in the audience feel seen, heard, understood.

I hope little kid me is proud of me. I made good on her

wanting to tell funny stories when she grew up. I became a writer and a performing artist, telling stories and sharing poems onstage. It took me many years to find my funny again. But if being a latchkey kid taught me anything, it taught me not to lose what's important, to keep making believe, to keep using my imagination.

So shoutout to the latchkey generation! We learned how not to be bored, how to invent our own fun, how to pair the citrus notes of Capri-Sun with the cheese and crunch of Doritos. We learned to stay out of trouble, and when we did get in trouble, we learned to make it look like we stayed out of trouble by the time our parents got home. We may have picked up some rejection and abandonment issues along the way but who cares, that's what therapy is for! Most of all, shoutout to Eddie Murphy and his red leather suit. I still haven't found a red leather outfit, but I'll keep looking.

MELODIES FROM HEAVEN

come from generations of church people on both sides of my family: Black, Southern, Pentecostal Holiness church people. Saved, sanctified, Holy Ghost–filled and fire-baptized church people. Preachers, pastors, and church musicians are in my bloodline on both sides. My dad was a young minister in the Holiness church and directed mass choirs. He continued doing this after enlisting in the Air Force by directing choirs at the chapels on various bases where he was stationed.

My maternal grandmother began playing piano as a teenager and traveled around North Carolina playing piano for various churches and choirs. A love for gospel music is deep in the roots of my family and in who I am. I sat next to my dad and my grandmother during their respective choir rehearsals, learning old hymns and songs written by James Cleveland, Andraé Crouch, and Walter Hawkins.

By the time my mom, my sister, and I joined a church community in San Antonio, Texas, it was the mid-1990s. What church folks would have called "secular music" was having a time. Biggie Smalls. Dr. Dre. Snoop Dogg. Total. SWV. TLC. ABC. BBD. 702. 112. Boys II Men. 2Pac. I rushed home from school to catch *TRL* and *106th & Park*. Okay, there were a *lot* of letters and numbers to keep up with.

My mom and the church folks started getting a bit nervous about what all this "secular music" was communicating to us as teenagers. My mom refused to let me buy Bone Thugs-N-Harmony's CD, even though I was very pressed to listen to "Crossroads" with my Discman. Christian bookstores started marketing an "if you like ______, then you'll like ______" strategy. This was my mom's favorite thing. "If you like SWV, then you'll like Trin-i-tee 5:7." "If you like Mary J. Blige, then you'll like Yolanda Adams."

Fortunately for me (and my mom and all the worried church folks), gospel music in the 1990s was jamming, hitting, slapping, boxing, bopping. Yes, it did all those things! The bass lines were thumping, the vocals were immaculately conceived, the drums were crispy, therefore I was at least interested in giving it a listen.

Then I joined the youth choir, directed by the auspicious Sis. Wilson. Sis. Wilson didn't play. There would be no chewing gum or chitchat in her choir rehearsal. Every fourth Sunday the youth were invited to sing in front of the whole church. We had matching purple polyester shirts with gold buttons that we wore special for the occasion. We could sing three songs, possibly including a march-in song, an offering song, a song right before the sermon also known as a pre-sermonic hymn, or an altar call song.

A march-in song had to be well-chosen. No games could be

played. No missteps could be had. The groove had to be strong enough to warrant 20 to 1,160 people marching in step from the back of the church all the way up to the choir stand. The song could possibly warrant a simple, mid-aisle dance move, such as is required for Hezekiah Walker's "I Will Go in Jesus' Name" or John P. Kee's "Never Shall Forget." This tune had to build anticipation in the congregation. It had to be either a song they couldn't wait to sing or a song they couldn't wait to learn just by hearing the organ and the bass line. The march-in song is how the church knows the choir means business.

The offering song needed to be a lighthearted ditty, something that cooed to the audience as they parted with their hard-earned cash and passed the offering plate. It also had to be a bit of a bop in case your church made people walk toward the front, row by row, because church members need the right groove to stunt in their best church outfit.

The song before the sermon, the pre-sermonic hymn, had to slow things down a bit. It's the choir's job to prepare the congregation for the word (*word* here could also be pronounced as if to rhyme with the word *void*—woid, as if pronounced by Credence Clearwater Revival). Here, you needed the equivalent of a worshipful slow jam. The bass can be a little grimy, the piano can be tinkered with, maybe a horn or two are necessary. Here you needed a soloist. Someone who tenderly grabbed the mic from the mic stand and unwrapped the mic cord before standing in place. Someone who whispered some tender prayers before they sang up and down the place.

The altar call song is a bit of improvisation between the choir, the musicians, and the preacher. The musicians have already joined the preacher in the last beats of the sermon. The organ is there to highlight a hoop or hasten a holler. The piano is there to pluck at the heartstrings of all of us sinners in case

God is calling our name that day. And if the preacher gets in the zone, the drummer has to join in just in case a church shout is needed.

The choir has to be prepared for anything: a slow, mournful song or a shout of praise song, and the choir is expected to have a song in the pocket in case the preacher finishes their sermon and someone else comes up to lead the altar call. In the church I grew up in the altar call could run for twenty minutes to three days depending on how many people needed to be delivert, so the choir had to be prepared for anything, including taking water and food breaks as needed.

The year I joined the youth choir, a man with a perfect fade, sharp side part, and flawless s-curl named Kirk Franklin released a gospel album called *Kirk Franklin and the Family (Live)*. A couple years later, he released the gospel album *Whatcha Lookin' 4*. If it weren't for Kirk Franklin, how would we know we could yell "Go Jesus Go Jesus Go!" or "Ain't no party like a Holy Ghost party!"? *Whatcha Lookin' 4* is full of hits but there is one hit in particular that still gets me every time: "Melodies from Heaven."

I've been a church girl for a long time. I've been a church girl who spent four of the seven days in a week at church. I've been a church girl who didn't even go to church. In so many ways, I'll always be a church girl. There are some things about being a church girl that only other church folks know or understand, but every now and then there is a church girl experience that transcends whether or not you consider yourself a church person. "Melodies from Heaven" is one of those things.

I sang "Melodies from Heaven" in church in the choir. I've driven around the city for a night out with a mix of friends who grew up in church and some who would never darken the doorsteps of a church, and the mood in the car shifts when you hear that bass line and keyboard at the beginning of the song.

Everybody becomes a tenor to sing, "Melodies from heaven rain down on me." Heads nod. Bodies sway. Shoulders bounce. Altos, sopranos, and tenors find their notes and sing. Sopranos call and the rest of us become the choir who responds. We enter a delicious three-part tag in the round. And we keep modulating up every time Kirk tells us to.

I've been with Black folks in a church, at a concert, in a club, and when the deejay spins this song the same thing happens every time. The whole room becomes a choir. The Baptists, the agnostics, the holy rollers, the blunt rollers, the queer people, the shy people, the church people, the cussing people, the people with a drink in their hand, the people who lift their hands in praise, for four minutes are in agreement about one thing. We all want melodies from heaven to rain down on us.

We might not be sure if we believe in heaven. We might have had some church folks say and do some shit we're still healing from. We might have said and done some shit we're still healing from. We might have more questions than answers when it comes to faith or religion. But, if there is a God who cares, who listens, we decide as our shoulders bop to that groove maybe we would like a God who loves us to hold us close. Maybe we would like some goodness to rain down on us, or on maaaaaay, as the song says.

We find a way to sing together. Some of us think of our grandmother we went to church with. Some of us remember our first church crush. We think of the people we come from. We think of Black Jesus from *Good Times*. Some of us think of the ways gospel music carried our people through all the terrible eras of America, including this one. When I look around the room and see teeth and smiles and blunts in the air and drinks raised and shoulders swaying, so many shades of us leaning our heads back to sing, I am reminded how much I love being Black; the ways Black people find home with each other, across religion, across generations, across the diaspora. When the music drops out and all we can hear is each other's voices and hand claps it's like for a few minutes everything is right with the world. And that is what I can only imagine is truly a melody from heaven.

A BLACK GIRL BLESSING

When I was growing up in church each service ended with a benediction, a blessing, a prayer for each person to arrive safely to their next destination, for strength, for peace, until the next time we met again. Sometimes, inside myself, I pray a Black girl benediction, a Black Girl Blessing, when I leave my friends, when I hug my sister, when I kiss my grandma's cheeks, when I tell my mom I'll call her soon. I've never written it down, choosing to let my heart freestyle it each time. But I imagine it would sound something like this:

I wish for you a Black Girl Blessing. I wish for you affirmations that arrive to you in the sound of Cicely Tyson's voice. The joy Cheryl Lynn felt when she decided it's got to be real. The beauty of Angela Bassett's smile and Nina Simone's cornrows. The hip flexibility of Salt-N-Pepa in the "Push It" video and the knee meat agility of Megan Thee Stallion. I wish for you the grace of Misty Copeland and the boldness of Angela Davis. I wish for wonderful opportunities to look for you the way Patti LaBelle looked for her background singers in that video. I wish you to only have to say your notes one time and see them applied.

I wish for you a seat at the table. I wish for you the tools to build your own table. I wish for you the tools to dismantle a table, a wall, a ceiling, a system as needed. I wish for you the wisdom of Maya Angelou. The electricity of Betty Davis and Rosetta Tharpe. I wish for you the swing of Olivia Pope's trench coats and the knowledge of when to pick up your purse and get the hell out of there like Annalise Keating. I wish for you the persistence of Fannie Lou Hamer and the sense of humor of Moms Mabley. I wish for you the hope that lives in the lilt of Whitney Houston's voice and the resilience of that dance Mary J. Blige does in her boots.

I wish for you the takes-no-bullshit attitude of Nikki Giovanni. The power of a Sonia Sanchez haiku. I wish for you the sharp wit of a Rapsody verse. I wish for you *griiiiiiiits* in my best Jill Scott voice and I will not argue with you about putting sugar in them . . . this time. I wish for you the commitment of June Jordan. The vision of Shirley Chisholm. The riotous love of Marsha P. Johnson.

I wish for you Erykah Badu's window seat and the need to never call Tyrone. I wish for you Edna Lewis's biscuit recipe and Leah Chase's gumbo recipe. I wish for you to be a keeper of the recipes. I wish for you hips that mapouka, wine, twerk, and tootsie roll. I wish for you that when Sexyy Red says, "Get it sexy," you immediately know she's talking about you.

I wish for you the bamboo earrings of an around the way girl. The giggle that beads at the ends of your cornrows can bring you. I wish you lemonade braids hanging out of an Impala. I wish you bubble gum bubble gum in a dish and as many pieces as you wish. I wish you the sisterhood Celie and Nettie held on to across two continents. I wish you the creativity of Missy Elliott, the foresight to know when it's worth it to work it and the innovation to flip yo thang and reverse it.

Oh, the Black girl places you'll go! I hope you go from traversing tightropes to learning how to float like Janelle Monáe. I hope you find your way back. I hope you find your way forward. I hope you find your voice like Mary Agnes at the end of *The Color Purple*. I hope you put your records on and find Black rainbows like Corinne Bailey Rae. I hope you find the strength, courage, and wisdom that was inside of India.Arie and inside of you all along. I hope you love who you are and who you are becoming. I wish for you to be listened to, heard, protected, cherished, and loved because *you deserve*. I wish for you the freedom and the joy to Black Girl in every way you want to.

ACKNOWLEDGMENTS

taps mic Is this thing on? Wow. Thank you. Thank you so much. Um, it is an honor to receive the She Finished Writing Her Book Award, and at the same time bestow upon someone else the You Finished Reading Her Book Award.

I would like to thank Black Jesus from *Good Times*. For loving and watching over me the same way he watched over the Evans family. I would especially like to thank my mom, Willa Jeanne Brown, who always believed in me and cheered me on and prayed for me. I am the writer I am because of you. Aren't you proud I made something good out of talking too much in class?! Thanks for being so proud of me and for ignoring every cuss word in this book. If writing ever makes me enough money to buy you a house, I will, but in the meantime, I will at least get you a pair of really nice shoes!

Thank you to my grandma Bertha Lee for telling her eye

doctor right in front of me that she was so proud of me for writing a book about her! You're not wrong, Grandma. I could tell stories about you for days. Thank you for being so funny and so smart and for pushing all of your children and grandchildren and great-grandchildren to be readers and thinkers and people who are curious about the world. I'll bake you a Super Moist cake anytime!

Thank you to my sister bestie/bestie sister Makeda Lewis for being the jelly to my jam, the Beyoncé to my Solange and the Solange to my Beyoncé. Mom really did her big one by giving me a sister and a bestie. Thank you for always nudging me to say what I mean and mean what I say. For always seeing me just as I am and loving me just like that. I love you down. You already know that.

Thank you to my husband, Matt "DJ Opdiggy" Owen, for the fifty-'leven times you had to hear this book read aloud over and over, the amount of days you got me snacks as I wallowed in writerly self-pities. Thank you for always believing in me and for being the first audience to most of my work. I still want to ride around the A, listen to Outkast with you, and kiss at all the stoplights. I love you.

Thank you to my literary agent, Margaret Riley King, for your patience and guidance. You told me to take care of myself, rest, and the book would arrive in its own time, and it did. Remember when I talked your ear off about being completely unsure if I could write anything longer than 60,000 words?! Thanks for not hanging up on me! Thanks for believing in me and making space for me.

Big thanks to my manager, Celeste Debro. I know you don't want me typing up a bunch of mushy shit and putting it here, but *you know how I get*. Thank you for being brilliant and innovative and always willing to learn and rethink and reimagine. I am better for having you in my life. Thank you for talking to me about business and about the proper way to fry fish and about a gospel song you just remembered. I appreciate you real bad. See, that wasn't too long! How'd I do?

Thank you to my friend and assistant, Leigh Kramer, for every time you said, "Fuck them," or "Fuck off," or "Fuck that." It sounds so eloquent when you say it. Thank you for your insight, wisdom, and encouraging words. For reminding me *no* is a complete sentence, and for really meaning it when you say someone is dead to you. You are the best!

Thank you to Phoebe Robinson and the Tiny Reparations team. Phoebe, your work as a writer, comedian, and producer is so inspiring to me. Thank you for founding Tiny Reparations Books. I felt at home and seen here, and it is an honor to join the list of fantastic Tiny Rep authors. Thank you for making room for Black women authors, BIPOC authors, LGBTQIA+ authors the way you do. It means the world to me.

Thank you to my editor, Emi Ikkanda, for seeing me and nudging me in such clear and gentle ways to write more, to dig underneath, to find my voice, to write an actual essay ending! Aren't you glad we worked on this together so we could talk about white refrigerators?! Thank you for helping make this book better and for making a strong draft stronger. I appreciate you!

Thank you to all my artistic homies who helped me keep writing and imagining and laughing. Thank you to one of my favorite comedians, David Perdue, for being a comedy consultant on this book. Please add all hours to my tab. Lol. Thank you to the homie and incredible poet, emcee, and writer Adán Bean for confirming and correcting many of my memories here and reminding me I got this. I'm doing an impression of your voice right now even though you can't hear me, but you will hear it in the audiobook version. Haha. So glad you are my brother from another mother for real.

Thank you to my friend and brilliant playwright Fran Da Silveira for commiserating and listening and asking me writerly questions. We see each otha but in a better way than Nene and Kandi did when Nene said that. Lol. Thank you to Austin Channing Brown for all them video chats and for accepting my random calls in the middle of the day. Thank you for every hair and writerly consult. They are both needed and necessary as are you, my friend.

Thank you to the homie Jeff Chu for commiserating with me over donuts and ice cream about why we signed up to become authors and masochists and allowing me to question my choices and decisions at so many turns of this book. I am glad to call you friend.

Thank you to Sharifa Stevens for taking my call about that one chapter even though we hadn't talked in years. Look at us, sis. *Thriving.* And I love to see it. Thank you to my friend and leadership guru Jo Saxton. Thanks for continuing to encourage me *not* to do a British accent and for always wanting fierce retribution for my enemies. Thank you for speaking life into me and for talking with me about *Love Is Blind* because that is really important.

To Kimberly Womble for keeping me up on entertainment news and for being the cohost of our own internal reality TV podcast that no one listens to but us. Best friend, thank you for laughing with me and always holding space with me. Thank you for sharing your shondo with me. Let's celebrate at La Parilla.

Thank you to my homies all the way from high school, Adrienne Howze and Michele Burns. Thank you, Adrienne, for always asking how the book was coming along and for having good words to say when all I had were cuss words. Thank you, Michele, for talking reality TV with me as if we really knew those people. Thank you both for talking through hair emergencies and booty music with me. Both are so important.

Thank you to the homie Celita for rocking with me all these years and for listening to my book reports and my movement reports. And all the other stories you didn't ask me to tell you, but I still did. Thank you for confirming and correcting my Spelman ministry memories. Let's do Legos sometime soon . . . or maybe you'll do Legos and I'll just talk your ear off while you do that? Thank you for being such a wonderful friend.

I would like to thank my braider Julia for getting me and my jumbo knotless braids through this. Thank you to my hairstylist Brandy Sims for somehow helping my edges grow and also snatching them at the same time whenever I see you. My hair is healthy because of *you* and I love to kiki with you. I'll have another story for you at our next appointment.

To my listening crew who listened in on the early drafts of these pages: Adán Bean, Adrienne Howze, Alisha Gordon, Autumn Lee-Cass, Asha Ivey Stephenson, Camille Hernandez, Camille Marbury, Candi Shelton, Celita Williams, Colah B. Tawkin, DaeDae Burnett, David Perdue, Ellen Kampinsky, Erica Odom, Gaby Arp, Helen Hale, Jeff Chu, Jo Saxton, Kimberly Womble, LaTasha Brown, Lisa Flick Wilson, Mark Kendall, Michele Burns, Nasim Fluker, Sharon Carelock, Sheree Greer, Shaté Hayes, Tanya Martineau, Varayna Cordell, and the whole crew at my Eddie's Attic shows in 2025.

To my dad, James T. Brown, I hope I channeled some of your sense of humor here.

Thank you to my family for giving me such great stories to tell about you. Big thank you to my cousins, aunts, and uncles on the Lee side for being so proud of me before you even read a word of this book.

Thank you to all of the artists whose music inspired me through this writing, including but not limited to: André 3000,

Anthony David, August Greene, Beyoncé, Cassandra Wilson, Chantae Cann, Dionne Farris, Eric Roberson, Erykah Badu, Foreign Exchange, The Gap Band, Infinity Song, James Brown, Janet Jackson, Jay-Z, Jill Scott, Kirk Franklin, Ludacris, Ms. Lauryn Hill, Outkast, Sisqó, Solange, Tank and the Bangas, Whitney Houston, and all of the music artists listed in this book.

Thank you to every reader of this book and especially to my Black women readers. Thank you for all the ways you Black Girl. Thank you for seeing me and giving me the opportunity to see you too. Oh and *girl*. Girl. Girrrrrrrrrl. Yeah girl. Exactly girl. Girl? Girl! Gurl. Gworl. And thanks for knowing what that means.

ABOUT THE AUTHOR

Amena Brown is an essayist, spoken word poet, and performing artist whose work interweaves keep-it-real storytelling with humor. She is the author of *How to Fix a Broken Record* and *Breaking Old Rhythms*. Her poetry was featured in the *New York Times* bestselling book *Rhythm of Prayer: A Collection of Meditations for Renewal* and her nonfiction writing was featured in the essay collection *Hungry Hearts: Essays on Courage, Desire, and Belonging*. Brown was featured in Olay's Face Anything campaign, was the poetic partner for PATTERN Beauty, Tracee Ellis Ross's beauty brand, and is a proud Spelman graduate. She lives in Atlanta with her husband, DJ Opdiggy.